USING CALCULATORS
FOR BUSINESS PROBLEMS
Third Edition

INSTRUCTOR'S GUIDE

GARY BERG, Ph.D.
Dean, College of Business
Western International University
Phoenix, Arizona

LEO GAFNEY, Ed.D.
Business Curriculum Advisor,
Author, and Educational Consultant
Lakeville, Connecticut

PARADIGM

ISBN: 1–56118–578–7

10   9   8   7   6   5   4   3   2   1

CONTENTS

TESTS

ANSWER KEY

INTRODUCTION

Value and Use of the Text

Like all Paradigm products, this text develops skills and concepts for the workplace. Proficiency in the touch system for the calculator, mastery of basic math skills, and familiarity with business concepts will prepare students for productive jobs and satisfying careers.

All of the students using this text have used calculators. But in the first hour of the course you will be able to demonstrate that using a calculator to add or multiply a few numbers is very different from using the touch system. A worker using the touch system will be five or ten times faster than one who does not use it. This increased speed means increased productivity, and employers want greater productivity because this leads, in turn, to increased revenue and profits. So the person who has mastered the touch system for the calculator will have a better chance of obtaining and keeping a job than one who has not.

Similarly, business and industry want workers with good basic math skills. Mathematical skills are needed in clerical work, sales and marketing, product development, and management. In fact, it is difficult to think of an area of office work or business that does not require mathematics. Often, the employee who can use math quickly and confidently is the one able to take on greater responsibility and earn promotions.

Finally, a thorough grasp of business concepts equips an employee to understand how his or her work contributes to the overall goals of the company. He or she is consequently able to interpret a supervisor's instructions, seeing the reasons for decisions and understanding the company's plans. This understanding naturally helps prepare an employee for a supervisory position.

In particular, this text and the courses in which it is used are required for entry level positions in any clerical job dealing with money. Calculator and math skills are indispensable for sales, payroll, inventory, purchasing, and accounting clerks. Since most students cannot determine the precise area in which they will be working, the math and business skills covering each particular job area are also part of the essential general preparation for today's workplace. The skills and abilities developed through the use of this text will also prepare a student to take full advantage of future on-the-job training.

The final three chapters of the text offer an introduction to accounting. These chapters will introduce students to some of the basic concepts and techniques of bookkeeping and accounting, thus reducing the anxiety level about a future course. These chapters are not essential and may be omitted depending on time or course sequencing in your school.

Course Description and Skill Development

This text is intended for an introductory course in the use of the calculator for doing business math. The objectives for each lesson identify the skills to be developed. The following tables separate these skills according to the three main areas covered: the touch system; mathematical skills; and business topics. When touch skills and math skills are not mentioned for a lesson, it means that new business applications are introduced while previously learned calculator and math skills are reinforced. As might be expected, touch skills are stressed more in the first half of the text and business concepts and skills receive greater emphasis later in the text. Skills and concepts for business mathematics are covered throughout the text.

TOUCH SKILLS FOR USING THE CALCULATOR	LESSON
Touch location of numbers by row and column.	1
Use of the total (*) key.	2
Use of + and − keys.	2
Use of the decimal setting.	3
Use of the decimal key.	3
Use of the 0 key.	3
Use of the multiplication key.	5
Use of the division key.	6
Use of the constant function.	7
Use of the memory keys.	8
Use of the percent (%) key.	10

MATH SKILLS	LESSON
Add whole numbers.	2
Subtract whole numbers.	2
Add decimal numbers.	3
Subtract decimal numbers.	3
Determine place value.	4
Determine the direction of an inequality.	4
Round numbers.	4
Multiply whole numbers and decimals.	5
Divide whole numbers and decimals.	5
Convert fractions and mixed numbers to decimals.	6

MATH SKILLS CONT.	LESSON
Convert among fractions, decimals, and percent.	10
Find the percent amount.	10
Find the base, when the rate and amount are given.	10
Find the percent rate.	12
Interpret and construct bar graphs and circle graphs.	14
Work with business applications of percent.	12–19

BUSINESS APPLICATIONS	LESSON
Weekly sales	1
Weekly customer totals	2
Sales by product line	3
Estimation of dollar amounts	4
Invoices	5
Miles per gallon	6
Weekly wages based on hourly pay	7
Extensions	8
Petty cash books and printouts	9
Checks and the check register	10
Sales tax	11
Multiple discounts, invoices	12
Markup	13
Revenue, expenses, and profit	14
Payroll and taxes	15
Prorating expenses	16
Sales quotas	17
Simple interest	18
Compound interest	19
True annual interest rate	20
The income statement	21
The balance sheet	22
The postclosing trial balance	23

Prerequisites

The only prerequisites to the use of this text would be the requirements that an institution might have for its initial courses "for credit." This text reviews basic math skills starting with whole number operations. Students who have mastered whole number computation will be able, in the early chapters, to concentrate more on the calculator and business skills. All students will profit from the material on fractions, decimals, percent and its applications, and the various financial forms and statements used throughout the text.

Performances

Upon completion of this course, students should be able to use the touch system method to operate a numeric keypad and an electronic calculator to meet entry level business proficiency requirements for both speed and accuracy. This proficiency, in turn, will help students (1) accurately perform accounting computations, including payroll, petty cash, check reconciliation, and inventory allocation; (2) accurately perform sales computations, including pricing (discounts/markups/markdowns), invoices, sales taxes, and sales quotas; and (3) accurately perform purchasing computations, including purchase orders, installment buying, interest rates (installment loans), and prorating (rental expenses).

Level

This text can be used alone or in conjunction with texts for business math, keyboarding, word processing, or accounting. It can be used in a one-quarter, one-semester, or ten-week core course or as part of a longer core course, depending on your curriculum and sequence. After successfully completing the course, students will be ready for courses in the next level of business math, introductory accounting, and principles of business.

Curriculum and Grading Suggestions

Students in the early stages of business courses need a good deal of support and encouragement. Consequently, we recommend that you carefully review the class work for each lesson. The various drills, applications, Apply Your Skills, Check Your Progress, and Mastery Checkpoints will help students learn and will assist you, the instructor, in assessing individual student progress.

The Mastery Checkpoints may be used to test students at the end of each lesson. Comprehensive tests are provided in this Instructor's Guide and are recommended for use after lessons 5, 10, 15, 20, and 23.

Product Highlights

This text contains three features that will help you teach and your students learn. They are: clarity of presentation, exercises structured for practical learning, and constant review.

Nothing bothers students more than the anxiety and fear that grip them when they fail to understand a new idea or procedure. It is these emotions that freeze the mind and make it incapable of continuing what should be an enjoyable intellectual journey. The only way to avoid this anxiety about learning is for the teacher and the text to present material very clearly, in small amounts, always based on previously learned skills and concepts.

The material in this text has been written, reviewed, and rewritten many times, always keeping in mind the importance of clear, direct instruction. Each sentence, definition, example, and procedure has been written in a way that will tell the student exactly what is happening and why. But, of course, the text is not intended to stand alone. You, as instructor, must work with your classes and with individual students as you present the material, in order to be sure that they are learning and are confident in their progress.

True learning usually takes place through doing. That is why this text has plentiful exercises. These exercises are not intended simply to fill up time. They are carefully sequenced to make the student active in what may have been passively received in classroom instruction. It always helps to have students do some exercises in class so that you can see if they have grasped the relevant processes and can apply them correctly. The exercises are intended to develop speed in the use of the calculator, proficiency in basic mathematics, and an understanding of business concepts.

One reason that learning often does not last is that it is not continually used by the student. Even in math courses it often happens that a skill is taught, practiced, and then put aside. Then when the skill is again needed, it has become rusty and is not available for use. Through constant review this text maintains each skill that has been taught. Exercises in the text constantly cycle through everything that has been previously learned. Thus it is not necessary to reteach skills frequently. If you require that students do all the exercises, then skills will be ready for use as needed.

General Instructional Strategy

This text is designed to support the teaching-learning process. When presenting a new skill, we explain the supporting concepts and reasoning behind the process. Sometimes a business or personal situation is described to motivate and increase understanding. Next, the new skill or method is introduced with attention to each sub-skill. Thoroughly worked out examples demonstrate each procedure. Then, exercises are used to transform passive understanding into active learning.

These exercises, as every teacher knows, are the heart and soul of the learning process. The exercises in this text are carefully sequenced to develop skills and concepts. Students move from basic math and calculator skills to applications, and then to extended business situations.

In addition to the instructional methods to which you are accustomed, this text will lend itself to the use of cooperative learning and study groups. If you are just beginning to use cooperative learning, you may want to start with short stretches of time. If you use cooperative learning for brief time intervals, it is best to use small groups. You might begin by having students in pairs check each other's work. Students in pairs may also be assigned to do one of the sets of applications exercises. Study groups, consisting of three to five students, meeting once or twice a week, can be a very useful way to review and reinforce learning.

About Calculators

Students taking this course will be familiar with calculators but many will not have calculator skills beyond computing with the four basic operations while looking at the keys. During the first days of the course you should show some of the different kinds of business calculators that you have available. Point out the difference between printing and display calculators and the advantages of each. Explain some of the special features and why one type of calculator might be preferable to another for specific tasks. The following paragraphs mention particular aspects of calculators that should be addressed as you proceed through the course.

Explain how calculators differ regarding subtotals. Display calculators show subtotals automatically. Printing calculators show only the numbers entered; subtotals and totals appear only when the appropriate key is pressed.

Point out to students the different registers or modes of operation within a calculator. In addition to the calculating register present in all calculators, business calculators contain an independent memory register. Most business calculators have an accumulating memory; that is, the memory functions as an adding device separate from the calculating register. Numbers stored in memory are added or subtracted to form a memory total. Students find it helpful to picture the memory almost as a different calculator.

After a general introduction to calculators and a look at different models, students should learn the details of the calculators that they will be using most of the time. If all of those in the class will be using the same model calculator, you can describe the features and functions to the whole class. If not, you will want to describe the different calculators to the small groups using each model.

The constant key, switch, or mode has many varieties in different calculators. Be sure to explain thoroughly how the constant function works for the calculators your students are using. Mention also some of the differences among calculators so that students will not be stymied or anxious when they come to a model in the workplace that is different from the one on which they have learned. Business machines are constantly changing, and employers want people who can use manuals to become proficient with a new model. For this reason, it is a very worthwhile experience for you to go through a manual with students showing them examples of each procedure. For example, on some machines the constant is the first number entered after the key is pressed, on others it is the second.

The use of the decimal selector switch is easy to use but students should be aware of the use of significant digits and the fact that in a practical problem an answer cannot be more accurate than the starting numbers. In the text, the direction line for problem sets gives students a decimal setting. But you should sometimes take a minute to discuss why the recommended setting is appropriate.

Explain to students how the clear keys are used. Be sure to note the difference between the clear key and the clear error key.

The Touch System

Explain to students that mastery of the touch system leads to outcomes much in demand in the workplace. These include: increased speed and accuracy; fewer mistakes; and keying confidence that permits increased attention to problem solving.

This text facilitates mastery through a step by step introduction to the numeric keypad. For initial practice, the keypad is divided horizontally into rows, vertically into columns, and into quadrants. Each number combination is covered many times in the exercises.

Home Row. You should first present the home row: the 4, 5, and 6 keys. Usually there is a touch marker on the 5 key. Have students place their first, second, and third fingers on the 4-5-6 keys. Fingers should "float" above the keys, touching them lightly. At first some students may enter numbers unintentionally because their position on the home keys is too heavy.

When students have become familiar with the home row position, you should teach them the correct reach to the total, the + and/or the = keys. This reach should be done with the little finger. Since the position of these keys varies, you will have to determine the reach and then instruct students about its execution. Fingers should remain on the home row keys while the little finger makes the reach.

Go through the home row drill with your students. A good technique is to begin by reading the numbers of the drill out loud. Have students enter the numbers as you dictate. In this way, they will be able to look at the keys if necessary. As soon as possible have students enter while reading the numbers themselves. Emphasize that students should learn to use the keypad by touch alone. Their eyes should be on the problem sheet, not on the keypad.

Top and Bottom Rows. Mastery of the home row is followed by work on the top and bottom rows. Watch closely to be sure that students always return their fingers to the home row keys. Special care is needed when working with the top and bottom rows. For a few drills you might say, "seven, return; eight, return; nine, return." After a few drills of this sort, students will begin to say "return" to themselves.

Columns. Mastery of the rows is followed by work with each column. These drills concentrate on one finger at a time, perfecting speed and accuracy while performing the necessary reaches. Finally, the diagonal drills consolidate and expand touch mastery before working randomly with the digits 1 through 9.

The final keys learned are the zero (0) and decimal (.). They will require practice, and should be reviewed from time to time. The drill for these keys is combined with a review of reaches for the entire numeric keypad.

Function Keys. The touch system as presented and drilled in the text emphasizes mastery of the numeric keypad. Students must also master use of the function keys. Of these, addition is by far the most important because it is the most commonly used in business applications. Placement of the other function keys varies with calculator models and so will have to be taught according to the machines you are using.

Errors. There are a variety of sources of errors. We will mention a few and indicate possible remedies. *Simple errors* in keying, that follow no particular pattern, are generally the result of carelessness or an attempt to work too quickly. Insist that students at first work slowly and accurately. Students sometimes *transpose*, keying, for example, 1386 instead of 1368. This error is usually caused by hurrying. Although, once in a great while, it may be caused by the visual disorder, dyslexia. Errors often result from fingers that have strayed from the *home row*. Use of the *decimal switch* and incorrect entry for the "add" mode sometimes result in errors. Most systematic errors will be uncovered through a careful review of the answers to the exercises. Sometimes you will want to check a particular student's work by looking at the tape from his or her calculator work.

LESSON BY LESSON INSTRUCTION

Classroom Instruction

A typical class might proceed as follows.

1. Write the assignment for the next class on the board and ask students to note it down.

2. You may want to start with a brief quiz or warm-up activity stressing touch skills, a mathematical procedure, or a business topic.

3. Review several problems from the previous assignment. You might do this yourself on the chalkboard; ask a student to come to the front of the room and explain them; or call on students for the answers and entertain questions.

4. Present the material for the class. This should be done with the aid of the examples in the text and other examples that you might devise yourself.

5. Encourage students to ask questions and discuss the topics presented. There will almost always be some students who do not fully understand what you have explained. Even those who do understand the material will make it more useful to themselves if they discuss it and look for connections with previous learning.

6. Assign exercises to be done in class. These might be done individually or in small groups. Move from one individual to another or from group to group and help those who are having difficulties.

7. Many classes should conclude with a 5-minute speed drill.

Lesson 1: The Touch System: Addition by Rows and Columns.

Be sure to stress the three-fold nature of the course. Students will be (1) learning the touch system of using the calculator; (2) refreshing their math skills; and (3) learning a variety of business applications. Most students will enjoy practicing on the home row and using the calculator by touch alone. Students should complete every exercise in lesson 1. Early and complete mastery of the touch system will assure success with the math skills and business applications that follow.

Encourage students to read the text. If time permits, encourage questions or have a brief discussion about new concepts and skills. Have students take a good look at the positions of the numbers on the calculator keys. Then ask them to close their books and draw the key positions. This will help fix the numbers in the memory, and the touch system will be easier to learn. As a related test of memory, you might ask students to draw the positions of the numbers on a touch-tone telephone. They are not the same as on a calculator.

Addends and a few other mathematical terms are introduced in lesson 1. In general, we have used only those mathematical terms that are necessary. So, those terms that are introduced should be discussed and reviewed.

The first set of exercises covers only the home row and contains many repeat numbers. Doing it will be easy, and students will see right away that they can in fact use the touch system.

Move about the room and check on students' work. Posture, finger position, and keeping eyes on the exercises are all important. Using the correct fundamentals will ensure progress later. Again, be sure students do all of the exercises in lesson 1.

Mastery of the touch system can be inhibited by the constant interruption of writing answers. For this reason it is advisable that students use a printing calculator and copy their answers from the tape to the answer tab. If this is not possible, you might have students do the touch drills in pairs as follows. One student does the exercises and recites each answer. The second student writes down the answers for the first student. Then they reverse roles.

Lesson 2: The Touch System: Addition and Subtraction of Whole Numbers.

Stress correct finger position and return to the home row as students practice addition of whole numbers. Emphasis on the diagonals will help develop the necessary reach while gradually developing the muscle memory. The first few lessons should be aimed at developing students' comfort and confidence in using the touch system.

The subtraction key is introduced in lesson 2. Students should try hard to develop the sense and touch of where the addition and subtraction keys are. But at first they will probably have to look frequently.

Be sure to have students check their answers for correctness. Ask them to do their own error analysis and perhaps write you a brief explanatory note if they have more then a few mistakes. You might suggest that they consider working more slowly. Students who have made a large number of mistakes should probably do the exercises over.

Lesson 3: Calculating with Decimal Numbers: Addition and Subtraction.

Take some time to explain the use of the decimal switch. Students should automatically note the position of the switch whenever they begin to use the calculator. Some may want to leave the selector set for full decimal display. But this is really inefficient in that it leaves rounding to the student, which takes extra time.

The A mode is an important setting. Be sure to go through several examples. Some of your students will have used cash registers or calculators in a retail store. They will see the value of the A mode. Be sure to stress the necessity of entering 00 for whole dollar amounts.

Lesson 4: Place Value and Rounding.

This lesson reviews several concepts important in business math. If, after the initial material is explained, your students are still uncertain about place value, you might show how numbers are built up in our decimal system. For example,

$3,426.15 = (3 \times 1,000) + (4 \times 100) + (2 \times 10) + 6 + (1 \times 0.1) + (5 \times 0.01)$

The placement of each digit means that it is multiplied by a particular power of 10. For additional practice you can assign exercises such as, "write a number with 5 in the ten-thousands place and 4 in the hundredths place." Remind students of the difference between hundreds and hundredths, and other similar amounts.

If some students have trouble comparing numbers, ask them to read the numbers out loud and then consider the place values one at a time.

Point out the importance of rounding and, if time permits, collect some examples from newspapers and magazines to show how frequently this technique is used. Discuss with students the difference between rounding and estimating. A company's revenue or profit figures might be rounded in a newspaper article, while the company keeps track of these figures exactly. But a police estimate of the size of a crowd is simply an estimate. No exact figure exists.

Lesson 5: Multiplication of Whole Numbers and Decimals.

It is likely that some of your students will still not know the basic multiplication facts. You might have such students construct a table with the numbers from 1 to 10 across the top and down the left side. They should then fill in all the products. Suggest that they study this table at odd moments and perhaps quiz one another. But we do not recommend that you spend much class time on the basic multiplication facts.

Help your students develop a number sense when multiplying. For example, a student should see that 6.6 x 7.7 will give an answer something like 6 x 7. Knowing this will help students recognize wrong answers that may result from mistakes in keying the decimal point.

Lesson 6: Division of Whole Numbers and Decimals.

Division with the use of the calculator is no more difficult than addition or subtraction. But you will want to review the basic concept of division so that students understand what they are doing and when they should use division.

Fractions occur often enough in business problems and in everyday life to make a review useful. The calculator is usually helpful in problems containing fractions. Explain to students that any fraction can be converted to a decimal and very often the decimal will be easier to use. The exercises on conversion and ordering are intended to increase students' familiarity and comfort in moving back and forth between fractions and decimals. Students should be able to work with any fraction or mixed number. They should be familiar with many of the decimal equivalents for fractions with denominators 2, 3, 4, 5, 8, 10, and 100.

You may wish to spend extra time on the business application for this lesson. Miles per gallon is an example of ratio, a mathematical concept frequently used in business and many other areas of applied mathematics.

Lesson 7: Use of the Constant.

The constant is a very useful function in business mathematics. For extensions on invoices, hourly pay, and a variety of other applications, use of the constant can save time. The constant is not difficult to use, but calculators vary, so it is not possible to give complete details about employing the constant. This will provide a good opportunity for you to read the calculator manual with your students and then go through the use of the constant step by step.

Lesson 8: Use of the Memory Keys.

Memory is another calculator feature that is used frequently in business applications. Since it also varies depending on the model calculator in use, you should read your manual carefully and then explain the method, using examples, to your students. The memory is particularly useful in applications that include subtotals.

Lesson 9: Petty Cash and Banking.

This lesson is devoted to extended applications. The petty cash book offers an opportunity for students to work with a computer spreadsheet—either by using the forms presented in the text or at the computer itself. If students have already used spreadsheets, this lesson will work well as a review. If this is the first encounter with spreadsheets, it will be an easy-to-follow introduction. In fact, you do not need to talk about spreadsheets at all. If you wish, you can simply treat the petty cash book as a table of expenses.

Most of your students will be familiar with checks and the use of a check register. But time will be well spent reviewing how to write a check, how to record the amount in the check register, and how to compute the register balance after each transaction.

Lesson 10: The Meaning of Percent.

Percent is probably the most commonly used concept in the mathematics of business and consumerism. When we say that statistics surround us, it is usually percentages that we have in mind. Whether we are discussing the cost of benefits, company profits, wage increases, or the allocation of expenses, percent is the method of stating the relationship. If students achieve thorough mastery of the concepts and procedures associated with percent, they will be positioned to understand a great deal of basic business statistics. As an instructor, you will do well to review a percent problem every day from the beginning of lesson 10 until the end of the course.

When learning or reviewing percent it helps to use visual and other models. The grid in the text shows one-quarter, which is equal to 25%. Ask your students for other examples of 25%: a quarter of a dollar; 15 minutes out of an hour; three months out of a year. A discussion of various meanings of 10% in terms of distance, area, volume, money, and time will also help reinforce the basic concept that percent refers to a relationship that can be applied in many different situations.

The percent triangle introduced in this lesson can be a helpful aid to students. In setting up the triangle we have deliberately avoided the terms percent and percentage. These terms must be used and understood, but for calculations it is best if the terms are then converted to those we use in the text, namely: *amount*, *base*, and *rate*.

Help students to understand the meaning of each term and the relationships. The *amount* is the number you are looking for when responding to the statement, "Find 20% of $450." The *base* is the number that you look for in answering the statement, "If you need $140 per month for food and this should be 20% of your wages, what must your wages be?" The *rate* is the number with the percent sign after it. Rate is the number looked for in the question, "If gross wages were $485 and the amount withheld was $105, what percentage was withheld?" Percent and percentage are sometimes used interchangeably, so it is important that students read each problem carefully and convert the terms to those in the percent triangle.

As explained in the text, the percent triangle is really a method for using the percent equation: Amount = Base x Rate. Base and rate are next to each other and therefore are multiplied. The advantage of having the rate in the second position is that students can use the percent key.

The percent equation can be transformed to find base or rate by simply dividing both sides to form a new equation. Thus, Base = Amount ÷ Rate and Rate = Amount ÷ Base. Again, the triangle will help students remember these relationships. The amount is on top and is the numerator (dividend) in each case. The rate or base is the denominator (divisor).

The fraction, decimal, percent conversions in lesson 10 are another means of building and reinforcing the concepts and skills associated with percent. The conversion table should be carefully reviewed in class.

Lesson 11: Discount.

This lesson contains the most realistic business applications used thus far. It offers students the chance to work with percent as used in discount and sales tax. Be sure that students understand each step as they proceed through the invoice calculations and that they check their work.

This lesson also introduces discount terms. Be sure to give examples of how to use the terms and then how to compute different discounts resulting from the terms. If, for example, terms are "3/10, 2/20, n/30" and an item is purchased on May 1, ask for examples of dates on which the different discounts would apply.

Lesson 12: Multiple Discounts.

The first example is on the calculation of rate when amount and base are given. It will be useful to review the percent triangle and again explain the meaning and use of the different symbols.

Once students understand how to calculate discounts, multiple discounts should not present any particular difficulty. But you should demonstrate different methods of saving time through the more efficient use of key strokes. The complementary method of calculating percent is one such time saver. This method will also help reinforce the meaning of percent. Explain that 20% off a price means that an item sells for 80% of the original price. The complementary method is particularly useful when working with successive discounts. For example, a discount of 10% followed by a discount of 15% on an item originally selling for $120 would require two parts with two steps in each part: multiplication and subtraction; followed by another multiplication and subtraction. But using complementary percents we have: 120 x 90% x 85%, and this gives the answer.

Lesson 13: Markup.

Many students find markup to be a tricky concept. This is, in part, because markup can be based either on the cost to the retailer or on the retailer's selling price. In the first case, an item can be marked up by any percentage. If an item costs the retailer $50 and is then sold for $75, the markup is $25 and the markup rate, based on the cost, is 50%. But the markup rate based on the retail selling price is 33.3%. You might find it helpful to return to the percent triangle and show the figures for the two different bases. Percent markup based on the retailer's selling price can never be greater than 100%

Lesson 14: Revenue, Expenses, and Profit by Division.

Graphics that give visual emphasis to presentations and reports are used daily in newspapers and in many areas of business. Pie charts and bar graphs are so commonly used that you should review them from time to time. These visuals also provide an excellent opportunity to review the basic ideas of percent. If the double bar graph presents difficulties to some students, spend extra time on it. You may ask students to bring in graphs from the newspaper and discuss how they are used.

Lesson 15: Payroll.

At this point in the course, students should be comfortable with percent applications. But you should take time to explain the details involved in payroll. Be sure that students work slowly, with a thorough understanding of each step. It would be helpful to have an oral review of the material in this lesson. Ask students for the meaning of rate of pay, overtime, overtime rate, gross wages, deductions, and the other terms used in the lesson. This material will also interest students because of their personal experiences with paychecks and deductions.

Lesson 16: Percent of Increase or Decrease and Prorating.

In calculating percent increase or decrease, students will have to be careful about positive and negative numbers. In this lesson we indicate negative amounts and percents by using parentheses, as is commonly done on business reports. You should take some extra time to give examples of how expenses are prorated. The fundamental concept is that expenses are charged according to sales; or that expenses are allocated according to certain percents that differ for different divisions or groups within a company. Discuss different reasons why one group might pay a larger share of expenses than another.

Lesson 17: Sales Quotas.

Sales quotas represent another common business use of percent. Once again, be sure to caution students about over/under amounts. Also advise them to look carefully and think about which number is the base in calculating each percentage.

Cost of goods sold (COGS) is a standard line on a business income statement. Students should understand the concept and how to calculate the cost of goods sold as an amount and as a percent.

Although these lessons place an emphasis on business applications, you should be sure that students are maintaining and improving their skills in using the touch system for the calculator. For this reason timed touch drills are included in many of the lessons throughout the text. It is best not to skip these. Since these drills are comparable to one another in form, they can be used to check each student's individual progress against the times of previous drills.

Lesson 18: Simple Interest.

Students will have used the formula for simple interest before, but it is important to explain each term and how the formula works because many of your students will be uncertain but may be afraid to ask questions. In this lesson, we use time in decimal form. You may want to spend a few minutes discussing this and asking numbers of months, such as 3, 6, and 9, and their decimal equivalents as parts of a year.

Lesson 19: Compound Interest.

Everyone is interested in money. This lesson can probably best be taught through references to students' own lives and how their savings can accumulate. If some students are uneasy with the concept of exponents or with exponential notation, use several additional examples of interest calculated repetitively. As a change of pace, you might ask one of your students to explain exponents to the class.

To help familiarize students with the compound interest chart, ask for the time in years that it will take to double your money at different interest rates. Then ask about tripling an amount.

Lesson 20: True Annual Interest Rate.

In this lesson we consider a type of loan in which interest is charged on the full amount borrowed even though the loan is paid back in installments. For this kind of loan the true interest rate is higher than the amount used to calculate the interest. The formula presented in this lesson can be used to find the true annual interest rate.

Be sure to explain to your students that not all loans or mortgages charge interest in this way. In many instances, interest is calculated based on the unpaid balance remaining after each payment is made. The section of the lesson on mortgages uses this kind of interest.

Lesson 21: The Income Statement.

The three lessons on accounting are intended simply to familiarize students with the initial concepts and procedures. The income statement proceeds naturally from the various business math topics that were presented in the text. Thus, although this basic business financial statement is often left until later in accounting, its introduction here will help motivate students so that they will not be afraid of their first accounting course.

Lesson 22: The Balance Sheet.

As in the previous lesson, this introduction to the basic accounting terms, the accounting equation, and the balance sheet is intended to show students that accounting is not mysterious or strange. Rather, it is a logical approach to business finances.

Lesson 23: The Postclosing Trial Balance.

The discussion of the postclosing trial balance rounds out the basic introductory ideas and processes of accounting. You should explain to students that there is much more for them to learn in accounting but that it all follows rules and procedures they can master.

Tests and Supplemental Touch Drills

Test 1: Lessons 1–5

Find each sum. Write your answers on the answer tab.

1. 879 987	**2.** 132 312	**3.** 456 645	**4.** 789 998	**5.** 645 544

6. 159 995 951 195 911	**7.** 735 337 575 337 537	**8.** 635 265 522 514 614	**9.** 758 774 458 887 847	**10.** 145 215 114 154 124

Set the decimal selector at the add mode. Add and write the sums on the answer tab.

11. 8.79 9.88 7.98	**12.** 4.65 5.46 4.66	**13.** 2.31 1.22 2.13	**14.** 8.25 5.28 2.88	**15.** 6.23 5.32 3.62

Round each number to the nearest unit.

16. 4.26 **17.** 21.8 **18.** 30.9 **19.** 199.5 **20.** 0.55

For the following invoices, find the amounts, the subtotals, and totals.

Midtown Hardware

Quantity	Item	Unit Price	Amount
7	gal. paint	$17.85	**21.** _____
16	brushes	6.95	**22.** _____
21 lb	soil	0.85	**23.** _____
24	screens	27.50	**24.** _____
		Total	**25.** _____

1. _____
2. _____
3. _____
4. _____
5. _____
6. _____
7. _____
8. _____
9. _____
10. _____
11. _____
12. _____
13. _____
14. _____
15. _____
16. _____
17. _____
18. _____
19. _____
20. _____
21. _____
22. _____
23. _____
24. _____
25. _____

Name _____

Test 2: Lessons 6–10

Divide. Find each answer correct to two decimal places.

1. 683 ÷ 15   **2.** 402.9 ÷ 23   **3.** 1698 ÷ 7.5

Express each fraction as a decimal correct to two decimal places.

4. 3/5   **5.** 3/8   **6.** 7/12

For the following: **7.** Find the total number of miles driven; **8.** Find the total number of gallons purchased; **9.** Find the average miles per gallon.

	Mon.	Tues.	Wed.	Thurs.
Miles	203	178	152	267
Gallons	10.2	8.5	7.3	12.5

Use the constant function to find the products. Find answers correct to two decimal places.

10.	406	x	10.5	**11.**	245	x	14.3
	309.7	x	10.5		4803	x	14.3
	486.1	x	10.5		30.5	x	14.3

Calculate extensions for the following partial invoices. Use the memory in order to find totals.

Home and Garden Products, Inc.

Quantity	Item	Unit Price	Amount
25 gal	w. fluid	$1.19	**12.** _____
23 qt	oil	1.26	**13.** _____
42 pkg	seed	0.87	**14.** _____
15 lb.	sand	1.56	**15.** _____
		Total	**16.** _____

1. _____
2. _____
3. _____
4. _____
5. _____
6. _____
7. _____
8. _____
9. _____
10. _____
11. _____
12. _____
13. _____
14. _____
15. _____
16. _____
17. _____
18. _____
19. _____
20. _____
21. _____
22. _____
23. _____
24. _____
25. _____

Name _____

Test 2 continued

Enter the following figures in the check register. Find each balance.

17. 2/1 Deposit $763.21, sales   **18.** 2/3 Pay $176.59, salary
19. 2/5 Pay $298.04, paint   **20.** Final balance

NUMBER	DATE	DESCRIPTION OF TRANSACTION	PAYMENT/DEBIT (–)	√T	FEE IF ANY (–)	DEPOSIT/CREDIT (+)	BALANCE	

Complete the following table showing conversions among fractions, decimals, and percents.

Fraction	Decimal	Percent
1/2	0.50	**(21)**
2/5	**(22)**	**(23)**
(24)	1.13	**(25)**

Test 3: Lessons 11–15

Find the discount and total to be paid for each of the following.

Amount	Terms	When Paid	Discount	Total
$ 2,000	3/30	22 days	1. _____	2. _____
$ 400	2/10	5 days	3. _____	4. _____
$ 290.50	3/10, 2/30	12 days	5. _____	6. _____

Compute the following multiple discounts and net prices.

List price 550.65   First Discount 15%   7. _____   8. _____

Second Discount 5%   9. _____   10. _____

Find the markup and selling price for each of the following.

Cost	Markup Rate	Markup	Selling Price
$4,508.60	35%	11. _____	12. _____
$7005.72	52%	13. _____	14. _____

15. Find the markup percent, based on the cost, of an item that cost $49 and sells for $75.

16. Find the markup amount of an item selling for $95 if it was marked up 30% based on the cost.

15. _____
16. _____

Use the following figures to find the percent of revenue by division and to create pie charts based on revenue.

Revenue by Division

East	$43,000	17. _____
West	$61,000	18. _____
South	$28,000	19. _____
Central	$51,000	20. _____

21. Pie chart

Calculate each deduction and (25.) net pay.

Gross Wages	Fed. tax	22. Insurance	23. St. Tax	24. FICA
608.45	57.20	1.7%	5%	7.65%

22. _____
23. _____
24. _____
25. _____

1. _____
2. _____
3. _____
4. _____
5. _____
6. _____
7. _____
8. _____
9. _____
10. _____
11. _____
12. _____
13. _____
14. _____
15. _____
16. _____
17. _____
18. _____
19. _____
20. _____
21. _____
22. _____
23. _____
24. _____
25. _____

Name _____

Test 4: Lessons 16–20

Calculate the amount and percent of increase or decrease from last year to this year. Use parentheses to indicate a decrease.

This Year	Last Year	Increase/(Decr.)	% Increase/(Decr.)
$43,200	$34,700	1. _____	2. _____
$25,400	$29,000	3. _____	4. _____

Allocate overhead of $23,000 proportionately to departmental space.

Department	Space	Expenses
Production	21,000 sq ft	5. _____
Marketing	16,000 sq ft	6. _____
Research	8,500 sq ft	7. _____
Administration	5,000 sq ft	8. _____

For each department, find the dollar and percent for over/under quota.

Department	Sales	Quota	Dollar Diff.	Percent Over/Under
A	21,340	24,000	9. _____	10. _____
B	56,290	42,000	11. _____	12. _____

Find the simple interest and amount to be repaid on the following loans.

Principal	Rate	Time	Interest	Repayment
$5,000	8%	2 yr	13. _____	14. _____
$12,400	9.5%	2.5 yr	15. _____	16. _____
$567.48	7.75	100 da	17. _____	18. _____

Find the amount each of each investment compounded yearly at the given rate and after the given number of years.

Investment	Rate	Time	Amount
$350	8.5%	5 yr	19. _____
$10,000	9%	18 yr	20. _____

21. About how long will it take to double an amount invested at 6.5%?

22. What interest rate will double $1,000 in 7 years?

Find the total interest, repayment total, and monthly payments on a loan for which interest is charged on the full amount borrowed.

Amount	Rate	Time	Interest	Repayment	Monthly Payment
$2,000	$10	2 yr	23. _____	24. _____	25. _____

1. _____
2. _____
3. _____
4. _____
5. _____
6. _____
7. _____
8. _____
9. _____
10. _____
11. _____
12. _____
13. _____
14. _____
15. _____
16. _____
17. _____
18. _____
19. _____
20. _____
21. _____
22. _____
23. _____
24. _____
25. _____

Name _____

Test 5: Lesson 21–23

Sales for Bill's Clothing Store were $203,700; returns were $7,340. Merchandise inventory on Jan. 1 was $23,500. Purchases were $140,200. Merchandise inventory on Dec. 31 was $18,210. Use this information to complete the partial income statement. Calculate the percent of net sales for the items indicated.

BILL'S CLOTHING STORE

INCOME STATEMENT

For the Quarter Ended December 199—

		Percent of Net Sales
Revenue:		
Sales	_____	
Less: Returns	_____	
Net sales		_____
Cost of goods sold:		
Merchandise Inventory, Jan. 1	_____	1. _____
Purchases	_____	2. _____
COG available for sale, Jan. 1	_____	3. _____
Less: Mdse Inv., Dec. 31	_____	4. _____
Cost of goods sold	_____	5. _____
Gross profit	_____	6. _____

For each of the following find the missing amounts.

Assets	=	Liabilities	+	Owner's Equity
$4,000		7. _____		$2,000
$45,600		$19,800		8. _____
9. _____		$15,470		$8,790
$57,200		$57,200		10. _____

1. _____
2. _____
3. _____
4. _____
5. _____
6. _____
7. _____
8. _____
9. _____
10. _____
11. _____
12. _____
13. _____
14. _____
15. _____
16. _____
17. _____
18. _____
19. _____

Name _____

Test 5 continued

Complete the cash account below by finding the balance after each entry.

Cash _____ NO. _____

	DATE		EXPLANATION	POST REF.	DEBIT	CREDIT	BALANCE DEBIT	BALANCE CREDIT
11.	5	1	Balance		4000 —			
12.	5	2	Purchase			750 —		
13.	5	3	Purchase			1900 —		
14.	5	4	Payment Rec'd		2500 —			

Complete the Balance Sheet.

Speedy Delivery Co.
Balance Sheet
January 31, 19—

	Assets			Liabilities & Owner's Equity		
	Cash		4200 —	Liabilities		
	Accts Receivable			Accts Payable		
	H. Jackson	750 —		Able Rental	3500 —	
15.	B. Okra	350 —		Taxes	2100 —	17.
	Equipment		14200 —	Total Liabilities		
				Owner's Equity		
				St. Marks Capital	9650	
				Net Income	4290	18.
				Total Owner's Equity		
16.	Total			Total		19.

Test 5 continued

20. The accounting equation is _____

21. Credits are written on the (right, left) column of an accounting form.

22. Accounts receivable is an (asset, liability, owner's equity) account.

23. Assets are _____

24. Name one possible asset of a company _____ .

25. The two most important financial statements are the income statement and the

_____ .

Supplemental Touch Drill 1

Calculate each sum.

1.	322	2.	987	3.	456	4.	252
	223		798		564		582
	113		132		471		174
	131		231		171		771

5.	25,632	6.	86,575	7.	46,532	8.	67,245
	62,523		74,597		41,235		71,273
	14,152		65,598		45,101		99,003
	26,412		97,504		21,254		70,402

Subtract.

9.	45,174	10.	95,614	11.	29,008	12.	71,263
	−31,848		−29,753		−23,232		−92,070

13.	584,602	14.	704,671	15.	506,812	16.	984,302
	−204,431		−456,102		−470,319		−675,280

Divide. Set your decimal selector at 2.

17. $17,091 \div 55 =$ _____

18. $17,098 \div 43 =$ _____

19. $287,720 \div 24 =$ _____

20. $909,670 \div 200 =$ _____

21. $45,781 \div 38 =$ _____

22. $8,093,670 \div 59 =$ _____

Find the sum for each problem below. Set your decimal selector at A.

Remember that each entry must be a two-place decimal.

23.	340.00	24.	270.21	25.	18.90	26.	85.30
	671.26		170.38		640.90		300.05
	7.00		813.00		50.00		340.10
	71.02		681.20		129.04		185.00

27.	581.02	28.	42.33	29.	89.00	30.	84.20
	478.00		278.00		106.30		57.00
	345.67		40.00		534.02		190.20
	89.01		39.04		58.50		59.07

SUPPLEMENTAL
TOUCH DRILL 1

1. _____
2. _____
3. _____
4. _____
5. _____
6. _____
7. _____
8. _____
9. _____
10. _____
11. _____
12. _____
13. _____
14. _____
15. _____
16. _____
17. _____
18. _____
19. _____
20. _____
21. _____
22. _____
23. _____
24. _____
25. _____
26. _____
27. _____
28. _____
29. _____
30. _____

Name _____

Supplemental Touch Drill 2

Calculate each sum.

1.	2.	3.	4.
213	132	466	714
332	312	544	285
212	456	798	396
323	645	978	465

5.	6.	7.	8.
67,332	16,575	23,532	7,205
61,805	71,997	1,235	81,273
14,710	65,183	5,108	19,473
23,562	18,900	24,264	43,452

Subtract.

9.	10.	11.	12.
45,074	45,874	26,068	71,263
−1,848	−9,755	−3,282	−32,670

13.	14.	15.	16.
614,602	454,671	406,012	884,381
−266,131	−176,102	−170,379	−643,200

Multiply. Set your decimal selector at 0.

17. 1,991 x 55 = _____   18. 98 x 43 = _____

19. 220 x 24 = _____   20. 670 x 200 = _____

21. 451 x 38 = _____   22. 800,374 x 59 = _____

Find the sum for each problem below. Set your decimal selector at A.

Remember that each entry must be a two-place decimal.

23.	24.	25.	26.
540.00	470.21	18.90	905.30
605.26	190.38	640.90	311.05
39.07	811.00	50.00	440.00
31.02	481.00	129.04	725.00

27.	28.	29.	30.
491.02	52.33	29.00	87.50
78.72	279.00	186.30	59.00
345.00	40.55	94.0	30.20
87.01	19.00	53.50	57.00

1. _____
2. _____
3. _____
4. _____
5. _____
6. _____
7. _____
8. _____
9. _____
10. _____
11. _____
12. _____
13. _____
14. _____
15. _____
16. _____
17. _____
18. _____
19. _____
20. _____
21. _____
22. _____
23. _____
24. _____
25. _____
26. _____
27. _____
28. _____
29. _____
30. _____

Name _____

Supplemental Touch Drill 3

Calculate each sum.

1.	465	2.	332	3.	456	4.	897
	554		322		644		645
	645		799		123		312
	466		898		321		951

5.	78,301	6.	16,735	7.	27,532	8.	37,205
	75,200		80,197		91,235		1,273
	21,994		60,123		85,108		17,253
	23,162		58,906		94,264		67,452

Subtract.

9.	65,074	10.	15,894	11.	28,068	12.	76,261
	−7,858		−6,711		−9,287		−42,690

13.	674,644	14.	494,211	15.	478,012	16.	804,381
	−268,131		−196,112		−381,379		−43,284

Multiply. Set your decimal selector at 0.

17. 91 x 95 = _____   **18.** 18 x 47 = _____

19. 30 x 64 = _____   **20.** 600 x 870 = _____

21. 41 x 35 = _____   **22.** 874 x 19 = _____

Find the sum for each problem below. Set your decimal selector at A.

Remember that each entry must be a two-place decimal.

23.	240.00	24.	890.21	25.	34.90	26.	925.00
	175.26		190.37		706.90		522.05
	39.74		716.00		55.66		448.64
	71.02		805.00		121.00		705.00

27.	491.00	28.	51.33	29.	89.20	30.	17.50
	79.72		49.00		106.00		54.00
	145.03		10.00		14.00		36.28
	87.00		19.33		52.60		21.00

1. _____
2. _____
3. _____
4. _____
5. _____
6. _____
7. _____
8. _____
9. _____
10. _____
11. _____
12. _____
13. _____
14. _____
15. _____
16. _____
17. _____
18. _____
19. _____
20. _____
21. _____
22. _____
23. _____
24. _____
25. _____
26. _____
27. _____
28. _____
29. _____
30. _____

Name _____

Supplemental Touch Drill 4

Calculate each sum.

1. _____
2. _____
3. _____
4. _____
5. _____
6. _____
7. _____
8. _____
9. _____
10. _____
11. _____
12. _____
13. _____
14. _____
15. _____
16. _____
17. _____
18. _____
19. _____
20. _____
21. _____
22. _____
23. _____
24. _____
25. _____
26. _____
27. _____
28. _____
29. _____
30. _____

1. 789	2. 456	3. 123	4. 311
988	645	645	788
321	798	897	624
122	997	554	486

5. 57,301	6. 26,735	7. 21,592	8. 7,205
79,254	20,757	94,231	61,203
20,394	68,323	80,107	57,293
93,166	18,986	25,260	11,402

Subtract.

9. 63,004	10. 35,894	11. 21,068	12. 16,261
− 1,838	−30,715	− 9,587	−2,630

13. 687,644	14. 304,271	15. 408,022	16. 504,681
−198,161	−186,192	−331,479	−73,288

Multiply. Set your decimal selector at 0.

17. 21 x 95 = _____

18. 13 x 47 = _____

19. 40 x 54 = _____

20. 70 x 90 = _____

21. 11 x 305 = _____

22. 44 x 79 = _____

Find the sum for each problem below. Set your decimal selector at A.

Remember that each entry must be a two-place decimal.

23. 160.70	24. 800.00	25. 54.90	26. 505.00
195.00	590.77	716.00	192.00
29.74	706.00	65.66	68.64
78.00	831.00	154.00	405.01

27. 403.00	28. 61.33	29. 39.20	30. 57.50
19.72	40.00	46.00	50.00
689.03	10.10	14.50	36.03
51.00	29.33	51.68	94.00

Name _____

Comprehensive Final Test (Lessons 1 – 23)

Add. Record your answers on the answer tab.

1. 195	2. 735	3. 789	4. 496	5. 349
915	915	321	104	753
551	571	717	459	648
951	139	303	270	691
911	535	828	159	502

Set the decimal selector at the add mode. Write the sums on the tab.

6. 8.04	7. 4.27	8. 2.00	9. 7.25	10. 6.93
2.80	5.40	7.92	4.76	9.00
7.00	8.63	5.10	3.91	7.61

Round each number to the nearest tenth.

11. 7.27   **12.** 21.81   **13.** 3.79   **14.** 19.55   **15.** 9.953

Calculate extensions for the following partial invoices. Use the memory in order to find totals.

Michaelson and Sons, Inc.

Quantity	Item	Unit Price	Amount
76 gal	fuel	$ 1.39	16. _____
41 qt	oil	1.06	17. _____
67 lb	seed	0.87	18. _____
90 lb.	gravel	0.56	19. _____
		Total	20. _____

Complete the following table showing conversions among fractions, decimals, and percents.

Fraction	Decimal	Percent
1/10	0.10	(21)
(22)	0.15	(23)
(24)	(25)	75%

1. _____
2. _____
3. _____
4. _____
5. _____
6. _____
7. _____
8. _____
9. _____
10. _____
11. _____
12. _____
13. _____
14. _____
15. _____
16. _____
17. _____
18. _____
19. _____
20. _____
21. _____
22. _____
23. _____
24. _____
25. _____

Name _____

COMPREHENSIVE FINAL TEST (LESSONS 1–23)

26. _____

27. _____

28. _____

29. _____

30. _____

31. _____

32. _____

33. _____

34. _____

35. _____

36. _____

37. _____

38. _____

39. _____

40. _____

41. _____

42. _____

43. _____

44. _____

45. _____

46. _____

47. _____

48. _____

Find the discount and total to be paid for each of the following.

Amount	Terms	When Paid	Discount	Total
$5,000	2/20	12 days	26. _____	27. _____
$350	3/10	5 days	28. _____	29. _____
$170.68	3/10, 1/30	22 days	30. _____	31. _____

Find the markup and selling price for each of the following.

Cost	Markup Rate	Markup	Selling Price
$3760.95	40%	32. _____	33. _____
$908.16	32%	34. _____	35. _____

Calculate each deduction and (39.) net pay.

Gross Wages	Fed. tax	36. Insurance	37. St. Tax	38. FICA
703.28	61.29	2.3%	6.5%	7.65%

39. _____

Find the simple interest and amount to be repaid on the following loans.

Principal	Rate	Time	Interest	Repayment
$7,000	6%	3 yr	40. _____	41. _____
$3,800	8.5%	5.5 yr	42. _____	43. _____
$310.82	6.255	200 da	44. _____	45. _____

For each of the following find the missing amounts.

Assets	=	Liabilities	+	Owner's Equity
$10,000		46. _____		$75000
47. _____		$219,800		$76,500
$21, 340		$15,470		48. _____

The two most important financial statements are:

49. _____

50. _____

Answers to the Text Problems

Page 7	Page 8	Page 9	Page 10
1. 1,110	1. 1,776	1. 444	1. 1,110
2. 1,191	2. 1,677	2. 543	2. 1,353
3. 1,029	3. 1,875	3. 345	3. 867
4. 1,110	4. 1,776	4. 444	4. 1,110
5. 1,191	5. 1,677	5. 543	5. 1,353
6. 1,029	6. 1,875	6. 345	6. 867
7. 1,110	7. 1,776	7. 444	7. 1,110
8. 1,191	8. 1,677	8. 444	8. 786
9. 1,029	9. 1,695	9. 336	9. 876
10. 1,029	10. 1,776	10. 543	10. 1,110
11. 1,365	11. 2,334	11. 976	11. 2,655
12. 1,335	12. 2,364	12. 976	12. 2,565
13. 1,366	13. 2,345	13. 965	13. 2,589
14. 1,345	14. 2,354	14. 986	14. 2,625
15. 1,357	15. 2,374	15. 954	15. 2,562
16. 1,366	16. 2,345	16. 965	16. 2,562
17. 1,345	17. 2,354	17. 986	17. 2,652
18. 1,357	18. 2,366	18. 954	18. 2,589
19. 1,365	19. 2,334	19. 976	19. 2,565
20. 1,335	20. 2,364	20. 976	20. 2,595
21. 1,653	21. 2,664	21. 666	21. 1,665
22. 1,677	22. 2,664	22. 666	22. 1,665
23. 1,654	23. 2,653	23. 655	23. 1,698
24. 1,665	24. 2,676	24. 676	24. 1,635
25. 1,676	25. 2,663	25. 667	25. 1,662
26. 1,654	26. 2,653	26. 655	26. 1,662
27. 1,665	27. 2,676	27. 676	27. 1,635
28. 1,676	28. 2,663	28. 667	28. 1,698
29. 1,653	29. 2,664	29. 666	29. 1,665
30. 1,677	30. 2,664	30. 666	30. 1,665
31. 1,965	31. 2,994	31. 336	31. 675
32. 1,995	32. 2,964	32. 366	32. 765
33. 1,964	33. 2,983	33. 347	33. 741
34. 1,985	34. 2,974	34. 356	34. 702
35. 1,973	35. 2,962	35. 368	35. 771
36. 1,964	36. 2,974	36. 347	36. 771
37. 1,965	37. 2,962	37. 356	37. 702
38. 1,973	38. 2,994	38. 368	38. 741
39. 1,965	39. 2,964	39. 336	39. 765
40. 1,995	40. 2,983	40. 366	40. 675

Page 11	Page 12	Page 13	Page 14
1. 1,212	1. 1,332	1. 719	1. 2,275
2. 564	2. 1,089	2. 995	2. 2,949
3. 888	3. 1,575	3. 135	3. 1,198
4. 1212	4. 1,332	4. 1, 668	4. 2,278
5. 564	5. 1,089	5. 35	5. 2,451
6. 888	6. 1,575	6. 887	6. 1,910
7. 1212	7. 1,062	7. 1,575	7. 2,754
8. 564	8. 1,035	8. 1,080	8. 2,296
9. 888	9. 1,332	9. 221	9. 2,487
10. 1212	10. 1,899	10. 444	
11. 342	11. 2,988	11. 176	
12. 432	12. 2,898	12. 2,563	
13. 408	13. 2,922	13. 1,174	
14. 372	14. 2,961	14. 1,774	
15. 435	15. 2,892	15. 566	
16. 408	16. 2,892	16. 3,927	
17. 372	17. 2,961	17. 2,802	
18. 342	18. 2,922	18. 2,604	
19. 435	19. 2,898	19. 3,018	
20. 432	20. 2,922	20. 1,593	
21. 2,322	21. 1,998	21. 2,485	
22. 2,232	22. 1,998	22. 3,632	
23. 2,256	23. 1,965	23. 1,209	
24. 2,295	24. 2,034	24. 3,420	
25. 2,226	25. 1,995	25. 1,002	
26. 2,256	26. 1,995	26. 1,420	
27. 2,295	27. 2,034	27. 1,675	
28. 2,226	28. 1,965	28. 2,457	
29. 2,232	29. 1,998	29. 1,726	
30. 2,322	30. 1,998	30. 2,642	
31. 1,332	31. 1,008		
32. 1,332	32. 1,098		
33. 1,365	33. 1,074		
34. 1,302	34. 1,035		
35. 1,329	35. 1,104		
36. 1,365	36. 1,104		
37. 1,302	37. 1,035		
38. 1,329	38. 1,074		
39. 1,332	39. 1,098		
40. 1,332	40. 1,008		

Page 15

1. 1,209
2. 1,677
3. 454
4. 1,676
5. 325
6. 861
7. 1,110
8. 1,599
9. 1,410
10. 948
11. 1,664
12. 1,685
13. 565
14. 646
15. 2,743
16. 2,025
17. 2,292
18. 1,686
19. 1,329
20. 1,341

Page 16

1. 1,220
2. 1,677
3. 452
4. 1,778
5. 246
6. 883
7. 1,107
8. 1,899
9. 780
10. 861
11. 1,656
12. 1,665
13. 656
14. 667
15. 2,735
16. 1,935
17. 2,262
18. 1,656
19. 1,932
20. 1,641

Page 19

1. 1,110
2. 1,272
3. 948
4. 894
5. 1,110
6. 958
7. 1,075
8. 1,111
9. 958
10. 1,210
11. 2,325
12. 2,265
13. 2,303
14. 2,285
15. 2,261
16. 2,261
17. 2,285
18. 2,303
19. 2,265
20. 2,325
21. 1,665
22. 1,665
23. 1,643
24. 1,689
25. 1,663
26. 1,663
27. 1,689
28. 1,643
29. 1,665
30. 1,665
31. 1,005
32. 1,065
33. 1,027
34. 1,045
35. 1,069
36. 1,069
37. 1,045
38. 1,027
39. 1,065
40. 1,003

Page 20

1. 1,837
2. 1,585
3. 1,684
4. 1,657
5. 1,882
6. 1,666
7. 1,585
8. 1,837
9. 1,387
10. 1,954
11. 2,663
12. 2,653
13. 2,654
14. 2,663
15. 2,653
16. 2,654
17. 2,640
18. 2,674
19. 2,653
20. 2,663
21. 2,993
22. 2,953
23. 2,982
24. 2,961
25. 2,952
26. 2,952
27. 2,961
28. 2,982
29. 2,953
30. 2,993
31. 2,004
32. 2,053
33. 2,025
34. 2,034
35. 2,055
36. 2,066
37. 2,034
38. 2,025
39. 2,053
40. 2,003

Page 21

1. 545
2. 383
3. 626
4. 545
5. 383
6. 626
7. 383
8. 545
9. 653
10. 338
11. 1,327
12. 1,277
13. 1,294
14. 1,308
15. 1,274
16. 1,274
17. 1,308
18. 1,294
19. 1,277
20. 1,327
21. 667
22. 677
23. 656
24. 690
25. 676
26. 676
27. 690
28. 656
29. 677
30. 667
31. 337
32. 377
33. 348
34. 369
35. 378
36. 378
37. 369
38. 348
39. 377
40. 337

Page 22

1. 1,110
2. 1,110
3. 1,110
4. 750
5. 714
6. 1,110
7. 1,110
8. 1,110
9. 1,110
10. 354
11. 2,985
12. 2,865
13. 2,897
14. 2,945
15. 2,861
16. 2,861
17. 2,945
18. 2,897
19. 2,865
20. 2,985
21. 1,665
22. 1,665
23. 1,709
24. 1,625
25. 1,661
26. 1,661
27. 1,625
28. 1,709
29. 1,665
30. 1,665
31. 345
32. 465
33. 433
34. 385
35. 469
36. 469
37. 385
38. 433
39. 465
40. 345

Page 23

1. 1,271
2. 1,622
3. 1,325
4. 1,361
5. 1,595
6. 1,325
7. 1,622
8. 974
9. 1,262
10. 1,334
11. 2,329
12. 2,309
13. 2,296
14. 2,339
15. 2,310
16. 2,310
17. 2,339
18. 2,296
19. 2,309
20. 2,329
21. 2,659
22. 2,576
23. 2,615
24. 2,649
25. 2,608
26. 2,608
27. 2,649
28. 2,615
29. 2,609
30. 2,659
31. 1,339
32. 1,409
33. 1,383
34. 1,369
35. 1,412
36. 1,412
37. 1,369
38. 1,383
39. 1,409
40. 1,379

Page 24

1. 949
2. 868
3. 625
4. 994
5. 562
6. 625
7. 868
8. 949
9. 886
10. 688
11. 1,992
12. 1,921
13. 1,947
14. 1,962
15. 1,917
16. 1,917
17. 1,962
18. 1,947
19. 1,921
20. 1,991
21. 671
22. 721
23. 715
24. 678
25. 725
26. 725
27. 678
28. 712
29. 721
30. 668
31. 1,001
32. 1,021
33. 990
34. 1,035
35. 1,020
36. 1,020
37. 1,035
38. 990
39. 1,021
40. 1,001

Page 26

1. 54
2. 205
3. 204
4. 166
5. 163
6. 96
7. 130
8. 71
9. 90
10. 102
11. 158
12. 597
13. 135
14. 366
15. 1
16. 208
17. 270
18. 9
19. 387
20. 72
21. 540
22. 346
23. 398
24. 78
25. 119

Page 27

1. 1,365
2. 338
3. 1,310
4. 1,186
5. 568
6. 543
7. 1,657
8. 1,665
9. 1,434
10. 948
11. 3,095
12. 1,685
13. 3,374
14. 2,022
15. 3,137
16. 2,135
17. 2,811
18. 1,622
19. 4,067
20. 1,579
21. 3,583
22. 2,811
23. 2,411
24. 1,053
25. 1,959
26. 2,020
27. 2,975
28. 2,727
29. 3,784
30. 2,375

Page 28

1. 4,137
2. 3,643
3. 3,387
4. 2,457
5. 2,617
6. 2,924
7. 2,515
8. 3,394
9. 3,464

Page 29

1. 1,587
2. 1,865
3. 1,490
4. 914
5. 1,920
6. 72
7. 177
8. 20
9. 99
10. 32
11. 1,269
12. 1,701
13. 1,669
14. 749
15. 764
16. 1,225
17. 1,212
18. 2,005
19. 1,976
20. 1,273

Page 30

1. 1,357
2. 1,555
3. 1,290
4. 890
5. 1,090
6. 2
7. 317
8. 91
9. 90
10. 102
11. 2,029
12. 1,221
13. 1,309
14. 489
15. 594
16. 765
17. 1,132
18. 2,505
19. 2,146
20. 473

Page 33

1. 60.005
2. 150.00
3. 240.00
4. .06
5. .15
6. .24
7. 306.00
8. 315.00
9. 324.00
10. 30.60
11. 31.6000
12. 32.4000
13. 3.0600
14. 3.1500
15. 3.2400
16. 6.0600
17. 6.1500
18. 6.2400
19. 90.6000
20. 91.5000
21. 92.4000
22. 120.6000
23. 121.5000
24. 122.4000
25. 15.0600
26. 15.1500
27. 15.2400
28. 18.0600
29. 18.1500
30. 18.2400
31. 2.1060
32. 2.1150
33. 2.1240
34. 2.4060
35. 2.4160
36. 2.4240
37. 270.6000
38. 271.5000
39. 272.4000
40. 6,000.0000

Page 35

1. 46.98
2. 53.28
3. 59.58
4. 13.32
5. 19.52
6. 10.36
7. 26.79
8. 19.97
9. 27.16
10. 27.12

Page 36

1. 33.30
2. 27.00
3. 33.30
4. 39.60
5. 53.28
6. 6.66 Sub
   13.32 Total
7. 3.36 Sub
   7.02 Total
8. 16.30 Sub
   34.87 Total
9. 18.35 Sub
   34.21 Total
10. 14.59 Sub
    35.03 Total
11. 2,154.83 Sub
    4,840.52 Total
12. 2,250.47 Sub
    4,711.63 Total
13. 1,988.73 Sub
    4,305.19 Total
14. 21,705.95 Sub
    40,202.53 Total
15. 22,222.47 Sub
    41,744.76 Total

Page 37

1. −1.01
2. −0.79
3. −1.98
4. −1.18
5. −0.99
6. 5.67
7. 2.40
8. 2.43
9. 3.06
10. 6.00
11. 1.89
12. 0.90
13. 0.20
14. 1.19
15. 1.89
16. 5.40
17. 2.94
18. 0.30
19. 2.70
20. 0.30
21. −0.54
22. 0.02
23. −1.69
24. 0.01
25. 2.69
26. 5.59
27. 0.18
28. 1.37
29. 2.48
30. 5.53
31. 1.54
32. 0.35
33. 0.88
34. 0.87
35. 1.22
36. 5.34
37. 2.12
38. 2.59
39. 2.83
40. 5.31

Page 37 cont.

41. 4.46
42. 0.02
43. 0.69
44. 2.01
45. 5.69
46. 1.09
47. 6.08
48. 3.37
49. 2.48
50. 3.43
51. 5.34
52. 2.05
53. 0.78
54. 1.07
55. 1.22

Page 38

1. 1,355.27
2. 1,313.29
3. 1,770.58
4. 1,809.59
5. $6,248.73

Page 39

6. Total: 644.21
   Total: 812.98
   Tot exp.: 1,457.19
7. Total: 500.84
   Total: 884.91
   Tot exp.: 1,385.75
8. $236.17
9. $78.50
10. $313.73
11. $93.81
12. $615.95
13. $70.08

Page 40

1. 4.50
2. 5.37
3. 14.69
4. 11.18
5. 3.45
6. 11.19
7. 3.45
8. 11.19
9. 22.01
10. 75.66
11. 53.42
12. 92.87
13. 798.86
14. 119.57
15. −14.92
16. 3,729.03

Page 41

1. 1.09
2. 17.24
3. 0.91
4. 12.36
5. 1.29
6. 138.48
7. 29.89
8. 151.82
9. 41.29
10. 8.14
11. 203.34
12. 30.33
13. 276.92
14. 915.20
15. 11.22
16. 201.76

Page 45

1. thousands
2. tenths
3. thousandths
4. hundred-thousands
5. thousandths
6. millions
7. ones
8. hundredths
9. tens
10. ten-thousands
11. ten-thousands
12. hundredths
13. 131.13
14. 911.591
15. 83.46
16. 125

Page 47

1. <
2. <
3. >
4. >
5. <
6. >
7. <
8. >
9. >
10. >
11. <
12. <
13A. 34.35
13B. 27.45, >
14A. 40.61
14B. 38.74, >
15A. 419.02
15B. 419.40, <
16A. 400.51
16B. 400.52, <

Page 49

1. 346,000
2. 8,946,000
3. 76,000
4. 3,000
5. 34.8
6. 1.0
7. 3.5
8. 675.9
9. 6.79
10. 40.01
11. 3.99
12. 0.09
13. 679
14. 1,267
15. 40
16. 5
17. $46
18. $7
19. $10
20. $1

Page 50

1. 81,659
2. 98,179
3. 182,284
4. 152,938
5. 977,427
6. 632,474
7. 1,774,734
8. 1,288,342
9. 1233.82
10. 720.49
11. 1306.82
12. 550.29
13. 1095.05
14. 162.50
15. 1,766.21
16. 1,530.31
17. 28.25
18. 14.97
19. 0.54
20. 73.02
21. 55.22
22. 78.91
23. 71.55
24. 51.92

Page 51

1. $15
2. $14.45
3. $4
4. $3.92
5. $30
6. $30.72
7. $15
8. $16.50
9. $20
10. $19.50
11. $100
12. $97.50
13. $105
14. $101.25
15. $300
16. $289.50
17. $50
18. $49.50
19. $360
20. $359.10
21. $240
22. $238.50
23. $540
24. $534
25. $1,440
26. $1,434
27. $380
28. $379.52
29. $500
30. $523

Page 52

1. hundred-thousands
2. hundredths
3. tens
4. ones
5. <
6. >
7. <
8. <
9. 56.6
10. 5.0
11. 78.1
12. 54.0
13. 122.79
   Exact
   122.8
   Rounded
14. 10.20
   Exact
   10.2
   Rounded
15. 6.30
   Exact
   6.3
   Rounded

Page 53

1. tens
2. tenths
3. thousands
4. thousandths
5. <
6. <
7. <
8. <
9. 23
10. 618
11. 10
12. 3,854
13. 0 — Estimate
    1.49 — Exact
14. −80 — Estimate
    −80.8 — Exact
15. 17 — Estimate
    17.2 — Exact

Page 57

1. 1,081
2. 4,428
3. 6,272
4. 1,800
5. 1,600
6. 1,458
7. 5,226
8. 2,640
9. 1,681
10. 4,056
11. 2,079
12. 3,808
13. 763
14. 4,980
15. 1,000
16. 1,404
17. 2,481
18. 1,748
19. 12,642
20. 35,216

Page 58

1. 9.00
2. 57.60
3. 44.50
4. 21.60
5. 24.00
6. 25.90
7. 4.90
8. 39.60
9. 0.30
10. 0.36
11. 0.36
12. 0.63
13. 342.00
14. 319.60
15. 533.00
16. 396.00
17. 14.50
18. 25.38
19. 61.64
20. 50.82
21. 28.35
22. 58.92
23. 41.49
24. 63.14
25. 400.95
26. 840.00
27. 167.28
28. 51.63
29. 206.15
30. 163.90
31. 684.50
32. 597.00
33. 55.80
34. 259.00
35. 230.62
36. 131.12

Page 59

1. 986.9069
   1077.9984
   611.4407
2. 0.0798
   0.6889
   0.7365
3. 1.1250
   8.4863
   19.8793
4. 307.4675
   2,619.2849
   892.1284
5. 851.2950
   30,213.3109
   24,215.9687
6. 164.4677
   1656.6831
   71,079.9884
7. .0606
   2.5816
   22.9842
8. 812.9690
   1164.7407
   3381.1258
9. 0.2746
   0.2251
   3.0366
10. 0.0134
    0.0006
    0.0006
11. 12.5857
    0.4465
    304.5577
12. 887.4230
    442.2473
    40.9831
13. 0.1068
    0.0433
    0.2344
14. 0.8004
    53.7477
    3247.9735
15. 0.0990
    0.3873
    2.6505
16. 4324.0140
    80,024.5271
    73,862.6385

Page 61

1. 202.80
2. 113.10
3. 774.00
4. 544.50
5. 1634.40
6. 548.55
7. 1770.00
8. 2524.50
9. 341.05
10. 5184.10
11. 339.75
12. 53.40
13. 82.50
14. 220.80
15. 696.45
16. 209.30
17. 99.00
18. 585.00
19. 209.44
20. 1102.74

Page 62

1. $113.80
2. 14.34
3. 39.90
4. 168.04
5. 441.00
6. 609.04
7. 177.30
8. 522.00
9. 127.95
10. 827.25
11. 147.00
12. 974.25
13. 64.75
14. 77.80
15. 11.25
16. 153.80
17. 101.20
18. 255.00

Page 63

1. 1,675.00
2. 3,008.00
3. 432.00
4. 7,440.00
5. 162.00
6. 433.10
7. 176.40
8. 330.00
9. 19.52
10. 44.16
11. −3.25
12. 1.60
13. 1.68
14. 4.94
15. 5.01
16. 7.24
17. 4.80
18. 0.82
19. 0.34
20. 5.40
21. 1573.25
22. 348.80
23. 1485.00
24. 3407.05

Page 64

1. 40.56
2. 58.88
3. 17.92
4. 0.22
5. 469.00
6. 753.30
7. $224.20
8. 491.00
9. 5,377.50
10. 6,092.70

Page 67

1. 46.72
2. 72.46
3. 180.54
4. 84.61
5. 21.61
6. 51.72
7. 27.55
8. 75.95
9. 841.74
10. 300.49
11. 129.67
12. 264.87
13. 315.60
14. 107.68
15. 250.00
16. 24.25
17. 104.44
18. 186.11
19. 3.10
20. 1.98
21. 39.00
22. 73.00
23. 38.78
24. 0.52
25. 43.14
26. 59.36
27. 22.53
28. 211.94
29. 4046.51
30. 941.47

Page 69

1. 0.67
   0.75
   0.63
   0.4
   0.4, 0.63, 0.67, 0.75
2. 0.86
   0.88
   0.80
   0.25
   0.25, 0.80, 0.86, 0.88
3. 0.56
   0.28
   0.40
   0.45
   0.28, 0.40, 0.45, 0.56
4. 0.74
   0.64
   0.50
   0.42
   0.42, 0.50, 0.64, 0.74
5. 1.50
   1.18
   1.43
   1.67
   1.18, 1.43, 1.50, 1.67
6. 3.13
   2.31
   2.10
   1.64
   1.64, 2.10, 2.31, 3.13
7. 2.50
   2.00
   2.38
   2.78
   2.00, 2.38, 2.50, 2.78
8. 3.50
   3.06
   2.51
   2.10
   2.10, 2.51, 3.06, 3.50

Page 70

1. 0.50
2. 0.33
3. 0.67
4. 0.25
5. 0.50
6. 0.75
7. 0.20
8. 0.40
9. 0.60
10. 0.80
11. 0.17
12. 0.33
13. 0.50
14. 0.67
15. 0.83
16. 0.14
17. 0.29
18. 0.43
19. 0.57
20. 0.71
21. 0.86
22. 0.13
23. 0.25
24. 0.38
25. 0.50
26. 0.63
27. 0.75
28. 0.88
29. 0.11
30. 0.22
31. 0.33
32. 0.44
33. 0.56
34. 0.67
35. 0.78
36. 0.89
37. 0.10
38. 0.20
39. 0.50
40. 0.70

Page 70 cont.

41. 0.15
42. 0.25
43. 0.35
44. 0.45
45. 0.50
46. 0.55
47. 0.85
48. 0.95
49. 0.04
50. 0.24
51. 0.28
52. 0.44
53. 0.60
54. 0.84
55. 0.03
56. 0.53
57. 0.06
58. 0.18
59. 0.17
60. 0.19

Page 71

1. 3.25
2. 7.33
3. 6.50
4. 8.17
5. 5.23
6. 2.08
7. 4.83
8. 1.75
9. 2.67
10. 6.30

Page 72

Totals

1. 1628
   31.0
2. 2344
   42.4
3. 1721
   30.9
4. 943
   26.5
5. 749
   21.9

Miles per Hour

1. 52.52
2. 55.28
3. 55.70
4. 35.58
5. 34.20

Page 73

Totals

1. 1059
   52.5
2. 1780
   143.1
3. 2153
   125.9
4. 1616
   172.1

Average Miles per Gallon

1. 20.17
2. 12.44
3. 17.10
4. 9.39

Page 74

1. 43.24
2. 150.88
3. 97.26
4. 77.56
5. 58.62
6. 22.57
7. 28.30
8. 43.48
9. 855.35
10. 281.96
11. 0.40
    0.75
    0.56
    0.57
    0.40, 0.56, 0.57, 0.75
12. 0.60
    0.63
    0.44
    0.83
    0.44, 0.60, 0.63, 0.83

Page 75

1. 260.43
2. 606.58
3. 446.16
4. 270.00
5. 77.92
6. 340.28
7. 500.70
8. 96.76
9. 406.91
10. 171.94

Total

A 2,435.90
B 2,355.42
C 2,118.03
D 2,761.57
E 2,189.09
F 1,946.04

Average miles per week

A 487.18
B 471.08
C 423.61
D 552.31
E 437.82
F 389.21

36

Page 79

1. 12,740
   10,430
   2,345
   7,315
2. 388.68
   1421.61
   1257.99
   78.718
3. 33.590
   174.53
   76.16
   334.16
4. 1.186
   1.460
   1.725
   1.548
5. 4.034
   1.977
   92.631
   34.767
6. 15.751
   4.948
   106.977
   331.475
7. 1,656.03
   936.72
   1,605.03
   624.03
8. 69.399
   9.616
   36.223
   7.164
9. 0.044
   0.312
   0.449
   0.401
10. 2263.26
    217.746
    165.100
    14.052
11. 175.00
    1,975.00
    5,650.00
    231.25
12. 10.8
    17.93
    387.72
    761.40

Page 81

1. $6.00
2. $7.18
3. $7.90
4. $8.01
5. $8.81
6. $9.73
7. $10.50
8. $11.83
9. $12.55
10. $14.89
11. $13.75
12. $15.58
13. $15.73
14. $16.22
15. $16.88
16. $17.75
17. $18.76
18. $18.94
19. $20
20. $20.26

Page 83

Total

A	7,869
B	9,196
C	5,737
D	10,519
E	7,868
F	4,239

Total

Week 1	9,529
Week 2	9,094
Week 3	9,275
Week 4	8,688
Week 5	8,842

Total

A	2,354.73
B	2,417.42
C	2,074.44
D	2,839.69
E	2,377.30
F	1,553.24

Total

Week 1	2958.48
Week 2	2638.07
Week 3	2635.45
Week 4	2647.73
Week 5	2737.09

Average Miles per Week

A	1,574
B	1,839
C	1,147
D	2,104
E	1,574
F	848

Average Miles per Driver

1	1,588
2	1,516
3	1,546
4	1,448
5	1,474

Average Salary per Week

A	470,95
B	483.48
C	414.89
D	567.94
E	475.46
F	310.65

Average salary per Driver

1	493.08
2	439.68
3	439.24
4	441.29
5	456.18

Page 84

1. 187.25
   147.13
   203.30
   179.23
   192.60
   152.48
   214.00
   195.28
   214.00
   184.58
2. 248.43
   238.88
   219.77
   184.73
   232.51
   216.58
   242.06
   251.62
   238.88
   226.14
3. 1,604.40
   1,105.89
   1,547.10
   1,294.98
   1,764.84
   1,598.67
   1,793.49
   1,426.77
   1,123.08
   1,243.41
4. 1,657.13
   1,752.87
   1,767.60
   1,244.69
   2,172.68
   1,885.44
   1,937.00
   2,135.85
   2,010.65
   2,312.61

Page 85

1. 62.10
2. 13.81
3. 155.25
4. 0.90
5. 262.20
6. 4.03
7. 313.95
8. 14.92
9. 193.20
10. 7.79

First total: 986.70
Second: 41.45

11. 176.25
    264.38
    130.43
    215.03
12. 104.89
    169.68
    89.47
    61.70

Page 86

1. 222.63
2. 24.46
3. 628.61
4. 246.02
5. 111.32
6. 462.27
7. 425.62
8. 324.72
9. 464.91
10. 275.80

First total: 1,853.09
Second: 1,333.27

11. 1757
12. 351.40
13. 168.2
14. 33.64
15. 10.45

Page 89

1. 49,542
2. 30,900
3. 21,891
4. 112,974
5. 27,277
6. 709,941
7. 584,660
8. 259,798
9. 1,087,521
10. 380,320

38

Page 90

1. 86.85
2. 373.59
3. 3,037.68
4. 2,095.95
5. 2,009.05

Page 92

1. 133.00
2. 179.16
3. 1,148.30
4. 274.61
5. 94.36
6. 161.12
7. 434.36
8. 604.68
9. 37.70
10. 312.21
11. 218.16
12. 767.52
13. 12.76
14. 201.18
15. 66.00

CONSUMER PRODUCTS INC.			
QUANTITY	ITEM	UNIT PRICE	AMOUNT
20 tubes	Toothpaste	$ 1.95 ea	1. _____ 39.00 _____
60	Razors	4.29 ea	2. _____ 257.40 _____
12 doz	Combs	1.45 a doz	3. _____ 17.40 _____
75 containers	Vitamins	3.60 ea	4. _____ 270.00 _____
15 doz	Pens	2.88 a doz	5. _____ 43.20 _____
8 boxes	Notebooks	24.75 a box	6. _____ 198.00 _____
		Total	7. _____ 825.00 _____

BOOKS GALORE			
85 copies	Cooking for Fun	14.95 ea	8. _____ 1270.75 _____
72 copies	Gardening	9.62 ea	9. _____ 692.64 _____
60 copies	Macrame	6.50 ea	10. _____ 390.00 _____
94 copies	How to Compute	8.38 ea	11. _____ 787.72 _____
78 copies	Dining Out	12.60 ea	12. _____ 982.80 _____
150 copies	Exercising at Home	7.95 ea	13. _____ 1192.50 _____
		Total	14. _____ 5316.41 _____

B & C FOOD STORE			
12 cases	Canned tomatoes	23.60 a case	15. _____ 283.20 _____
65 cases	Club soda	13.76 a case	16. _____ 894.40 _____
20 boxes	Corn flakes	19.65 a box	17. _____ 393.00 _____
85 pounds	Potatoes	0.45 a lb	18. _____ 38.25 _____
70 pounds	Carrots	0.29 a lb	19. _____ 20.30 _____
		Total	20. _____ 1629.15 _____

21.
794.75
724.63
729.30
500.23
897.60
640.48
841.50
546.98
701.25
790.08
7,166.80

22.
1,224.63
1,206.08
1,045.27
841.16
903.01
791.68
1,212.26
983.42
958.68
804.05
9,970.24

23.
1,269.00
731.79
1,226.70
1,125.18
1,302.84
1,256.31
1,323.99
1,053.27
829.08
917.91
11,036.07

1,928.75
24.
1,689.59
2,167.92
1,458.14
1,658.73
2,291.36
2,507.38
2,391.65
2,260.50
2,113.91
20,467.93

Page 95

1. 365.80
2. 134.30
3. 188.49
4. 591.40
5. 1.10
6. 623.75
7. 384.80
8. 338.00
9. 150.84
10. 441.00
    Total: 1,938.39

Page 96

1. 364.5
2. 26.02
3. 1.96
4. 187.70
5. 34.24
6. 573.00
   592.10
   595.92
   408.74
   733.44
   Total: 2,903.20
7. 1,465.20
   1,443.00
   1,250.60
   1,006.40
   1,080.40
   Total: 6,245.60

1.

	1	2	3	4	5	6	7	8
1	Received	Paid out	Date	Explanation	No.	Office Exp.	Delivery	Misc.
2	800.00		6/1	Company Ck.				
3		412.27	6/20	Brought f'wd				
4		48.10	6/24	Comp. Paper	223	48.10		
5		93.24	6/25	Disks	224	93.24		
6		9.50	6/28	Express Mail	225		9.50	
7		15.50	6/29	Fax	226		15.50	
8		10.50	6/30	Taxi	227		10.50	
9		17.88	6/31	Pens/pencils	228	17.88		
10		609.99		TOTALS		159.22	35.50	

Cash on hand ___193.01___

2.

	1	2	3	4	5	6	7	8
1	Received	Paid out	Date	Explanation	No.	Office Exp.	Delivery	Misc.
2	700.00		7/1	Company Ck.				
3		541.08	7/22	Brought f'wd				
4		57.91	7/22	Copying	311	57.91		
5		19.84	7/23	Disks	312	19.84		
6		17.50	7/26	Express Mail	313		17.50	
7		33.78	7/28	Bus. Lunch	314			33.78
8		23.00	6/29	Fax	315		23.00	
9		7.86	6/30	Batteries	316	7.86		
10		700.97		TOTALS		85.61	40.50	33.78

Cash on Hand ___−.97___

1.

	1	2	3	4	5	6	7	8
1	Received	Paid out	Date	Explanation	No.	Office Exp.	Delivery	Misc.
2	800.00		9/1	Company Ck.				
3		74.58	9/3	Comp. Paper	401	74.58		
4		21.50	9/5	Express Mail	402		21.50	
5		110.70	9/6	Software	403	110.70		
6		16.50	9/9	Taxi	404		16.50	
7		35.73	9/10	Lunch	405			35.73
8		21.50	9/12	Fax	406		21.50	
9								
10	TOTALS	280.51				185.28	59.50	35.73

Cash on hand   _519.49_

2.

	1	2	3	4	5	6	7	8
1	Received	Paid out	Date	Explanation	No.	Office Exp.	Delivery	Misc.
2	700.00		10/1	Company Ck.				
3		115.67	10/2	Cop. Cart.	501	115.67		
4		14.00	10/4	Delivery mess.	502		14.00	
5		97.24	10/5	Disks	503	97.24		
6		78.66	10/9	Postage	504		78.66	
7		11.95	10/11	Plant	505	11.95		
8		18.79	10/14	Folders	506	18.79		
9								
10	TOTALS	336.31				243.65	92.66	

Cash on Hand   _363.69_

3.

	1	2	3	4	5	6	7	8
	Received	Paid out	Date	Explanation	No.	Office Exp.	Delivery	Misc.
1								
2	750.00		11/1	Company Ck.				
3		98.56	11/1	Calculators	201	98.56		
4		29.00	11/2	Stamps	202		29.00	
5		39.75	11/5	Exp. Mail	203		39.75	
6		41.71	11/8	Bus. Lunch	204			41.71
7		19.36	11/9	Pencils/Pens	205	19.36		
8		21.00	11/12	Fax	206		21.00	
9		14.50	11/14	Cups	207	14.50		
10	TOTALS	263.88				132.42	89.75	41.71

Cash on hand __486.12__

4.

	1	2	3	4	5	6	7	8
	Received	Paid out	Date	Explanation	No.	Office Exp.	Delivery	Misc.
1								
2	500.00		12/1	Company Ck.				
3		44.20	12/3	Copying	301	44.20		
4		114.56	12/4	Postage	302		114.56	
5		56.39	12/5	Comp. ribbons	303	56.39		
6		9.61	12/8	Lunch	304			9.61
7		19.87	12/9	Film Dev.	305			19.87
8		27.50	12/11	Exp. Mail	306		27.50	
9		31.74	12/14	Envelopes	307	31.74		
10	TOTALS	303.87				132.33	142.06	29.48

Cash on Hand __196.13__

Page 103

NUMBER	DATE	DESCRIPTION OF TRANSACTION	PAYMENT/DEBIT (−)	✔ T	FEE IF ANY (−)	DEPOSIT/CREDIT (+)	BALANCE	
							760	00
							1713	27
							1502	77
							1408	14

Page 104

1. 3,582
2. 2,131
3. 880
4. 3,287
5. 137,041
6. 278,070
7. 177,689
8. 260,090
9. 56,757
10. 65,690
11. 29,433
12. −17,032
13. 419,481
14. 113,596
15. 294,250
16. 527,379
17. 88
18. 4,570
19. 2,778
20. 2,184
21. 861
22. 5,309
23. 1,475.94
24. 1,269.50
25. 1,199.88
26. 1,413.09
27. 1,556.50
28. 1,974.06
29. 1,864.94
30. 2,019.42

Page 105

1.

NUMBER	DATE	DESCRIPTION OF TRANSACTION	PAYMENT/DEBIT (–)	✓ T	FEE IF ANY (–)	DEPOSIT/CREDIT (+)	BALANCE	
	7/1	Deposit –sales				1780.00	1780	00
	7/3	Light bulbs	45.60				1734	40
	7/4	Repairs	119.87				1614	53
	7/8	Salary	415.28				1199	25
	7/8	Deposit –sales				2031.25	3230	50
	7/9	Furniture	341.62				2888	88
	7/10	Merchandise	1025.63				1863	25

2.

NUMBER	DATE	DESCRIPTION OF TRANSACTION	PAYMENT/DEBIT (–)	✓ T	FEE IF ANY (–)	DEPOSIT/CREDIT (+)	BALANCE	
	8/1	Deposit –sales				1546.93	1546	93
	8/1	Salary	509.87				1037	06
	8/2	Supplies	134.27				902	79
	8/3	Merchandise	764.20				138	59
	8/4	Deposit –sales				1287.41	1426	00

Page 106

	1	2	3	4	5	6	7	8
	Received	Paid out	Date	Explanation	No.	Office Exp.	Delivery	Misc.
1								
2	900.00		9/1					
3		45.78	9/1	Calculators	201	45.78		
4		19.20	9/3	Copying	202	19.20		
5		18.00	9/4	Fax	203		18.00	
6		23.00	9/5	Exp. Mail	204		23.00	
7		56.03	9/8	Bus. Lunch	205			56.03
8		21.00	9/9	Fax	206		21.00	
9		12.35	9/10	Taxi	207		12.35	
10		9.19	9/10	Comp. ribbon	208	9.19		
TOTALS		204.55				74.17	74.35	56.03

Cash on hand   __695.45__

Page 107

NUMBER	DATE	DESCRIPTION OF TRANSACTION	PAYMENT/DEBIT (–)	✔ T	FEE IF ANY (–)	DEPOSIT/CREDIT (+)	BALANCE	
	4/1	Deposit –sales				2950.00	2950	00
	4/2	Supplies	65.40				2884	60
	4/3	Rent	650.00				2234	60
	4/4	Salary	214.98				2019	62
	4/5	Taxes	605.27				1414	35
	4/9	Deposit –sales				1331.85	2746	20
	4/10	Software	256.09				2490	11
	4/11	Repairs	94.55				2395	56

Fraction	Decimal	Percent	
1/2	.50	50%	
1/10	0.10	10%	
1/20	.05	5%	
3/4	0.75	75%	
2/3	.67	67%	
3/10	.30	30%	
1/8	.13	13%	
1/100	0.01	1%	
9/10	.90	90%	
1/200	0.005	.5%	*(or 1% if rounded)*
2/7	.29	29%	
6/5	1.2	120%	
3/2	1.50	150%	
3/20	.15	15%	
3/100	.03	3%	

Page 114

1. 4.32
2. 10.54
3. 24.16
4. 34.43
5. 57.15
6. 73.03
7. 85.71
8. 121.76
9. 145.84
10. 174.56
11. 213.51
12. 298.60
13. 642.24
14. 1,096.89
15. 1,906.84
16. 1,525.57
17. 4,429.16
18. 52.16
19. 828.61
20. 407.02
21. 11.47
22. 16.07
23. 51.20
24. 4.28
25. 397.65
26. 190.00

Page 116

1. 27.61
2. 48.04
3. 91.24
4. 81.12
5. 82.33
6. 54.78
7. 81.40
8. 53.36
9. 99.74
10. 116.73
11. 107.94
12. 538.91
13. 81.81
14. 70.09
15. 67.24
16. 7.06
17. 128.80
18. 16.72
19. 71.62
20. 200.01

Page 118

1. 57.58
2. 179.17
3. 173.51
4. 162.75
5. 122.89
6. 122.67
7. 119.94
8. 230.60
9. 243.18
10. 1,036.77
11. 1,686.95
12. 1,552.79
13. 2,032.40
14. 7,718.06
15. 10,803.55
16. 237.22
17. 563.51
18. 9,064.20
19. 246.04
20. 74.10

Page 119

1. 688
2. 2,634
3. 1,503
4. 2,793
5. 89,228
6. 254,294
7. 225,510
8. 150,168
9. −41,674
10. 9,901
11. 76,566
12. 52,721
13. 529,231
14. 328,569
15. 36,500
16. 110,072
17. 1,742
18. 502
19. 4,435
20. 1,157
21. 655
22. 8,765
23. 1,147.37
24. 2,403.89
25. 838.84
26. 910.45
27. 1,493.70
28. 819.46
29. 1,327.80
30. 1.610.38

Page 120

1. $1448.00
2. 5
3. $250.00
4. 17,400
5. 34
6. 571,428.57
7. 75.02
8. 20
9. 4
10. $500.00
11A. 7.5
11B. 9.17
12. 14,388

Page 121

1. $100.58
2. $2.79
3. 15
4. $20.00
5. 14
6. 18.67
7. 48.67
8. $31.63
9. 5.5
10. 220
11. 46.5
12. 130.8
13. 9.28
14. $91.20

Page 122

1. 33.3
2. 233.3
3. $36.05
4. $45.70
5. $135.36
6. $54.55
7. $54.17
8. $18.37
9. 85.71
10. 116.67
11. $22.11
12. $15.00
13. $5100.00
14. 10,967,741.94
(10.97 million)

Page 125

	Discount Amount			Net Cost
1.	$17.40		1.	$417.60
2.	64.73		2.	798.27
3.	64.90		3.	584.10
4.	8.26		4.	118.74
5.	36.42		5.	1784.58

Page 127

	Discount			Total
1.	$26.76		1.	$865.40
2.	00.00		2.	304.50
3.	18.37		3.	594.07
4.	18.81		4.	921.47
5.	46.18		5.	2,262.58
6.	19.04		6.	1,885.32
7.	102.36		7.	3,309.69
8.	196.09		8.	4,706.11
9.	00.00		9.	6,209.56
10.	23.50		10.	759.79

1.	$3.50
2.	8.16
3.	10.22
4.	5.83
5.	$32.20
6.	2.28
7.	48.09
8.	12.04

Customer:

Invoice

Number: 15491

```
Computer Service Co.
14 West Drive
Service City, USA  01222
```

CUSTOMER ORDER NO.	SALESMAN	TERMS	INVOICE PAID IN:	F.O.B.	DATE
B-20144	Jason	2/10, N/30	30 Days	—	3/26

ITEM	QUANTITY	DESCRIPTION	UNIT PRICE		AMOUNT	
1201	25	#10 Bolts	3	40	85	00
1490	40	Fasteners	2	90	116	00
1678	100	Port covers	6	00	600	00
2347	67	Washers		49	32	83
0055	115	Brackets	4	08	469	20
0002	75	Bracket fasteners		67	50	25
1237	10	Chip sockets	1	29	12	90
		Subtotal			1366	18
		discount				
		Subtotal			1366	18
		4% Sales tax			54	65
		Invoice total			1420	83

1.	2958
2.	3450
3.	2202
4.	1896
5.	285,391
6.	136,243
7.	119,258
8.	322,386
9.	56,332
10.	37,912
11.	19,596
12.	−36,306
13.	554,434
14.	305,379
15.	−233,964
16.	−333,333
17.	307
18.	824
19.	1870
20.	1525
21.	2602
22.	17,015
23.	816.79
24.	1,203.37
25.	1,161.90
26.	1,194.72
27.	1,872.85
28.	1,228.57
29.	2,060.71
30.	901.00

Page 132

	Discount		Total
1.	$20.00	1.	$980.00
2.	22.50	2.	727.50
3.	9.52	3.	466.38
4.	15.28	4.	494.07
5.	00.00	5.	5,680.27

Customer:

Invoice

Number: 15492

Toyland, USA

720 Shopping Center Drive

Toy City, USA   01133

CUSTOMER ORDER NO.	SALESMAN	TERMS	INVOICE PAID IN:	F.O.B.	DATE
X-5022	Mary	3/10, 2/10, N/30	22 Days	—	4/1

ITEM	QUANTITY	DESCRIPTION	UNIT PRICE		AMOUNT	
0679	34	Mix-match small cars #490	7	20	244	80
0205	112	Teddy bear books #A21		98	109	76
0102	96	Plastic army men #A-111		29	27	84
0860	14	Dolls #624	4	77	66	78
7211	25	Combination baseball sets	1	30	32	50
0449	48	Card games		98	47	04
0668	72	Rubber balls 1" diameter		70	50	40
		Subtotal			579	12
		discount			—	—
		Subtotal			579	12
		4% Sales tax			23	16
		Invoice total			602	28

Discount		Total	
1.	$00.00	1.	$2,500.00
2.	24.15	2.	780.85
3.	5.72	3.	566.43
4.	16.91	4.	828.69
5.	159.00	5.	7,791.00

1.	$43.20
2.	$29.30
3.	15.73
	770.86
	38.54
	809.40
4.	156.07
	15,450.93
	772.55
	16,223.48
5.	2.5%
6.	3%

Customer:

Invoice

Number: 15493

Auto Shop, Inc.

1689 Engine Drive

Motor City, USA 01333

CUSTOMER ORDER NO.	SALESMAN	TERMS	INVOICE PAID IN:	F.O.B.	DATE
M–48321	Justin	2/10, N/30	9 Days	—	4/3

ITEM	QUANTITY	DESCRIPTION	UNIT PRICE		AMOUNT	
0043	80	Spark plug sets A465	2	29	183	20
0542	112	Regular size wrenches		98	109	76
0111	50	Auto shine polish	5	09	254	50
7010	40	Clamps	1	07	42	80
0009	120			98	117	60
0784	70		1	39	97	30
		Subtotal			805	16
		discount			16	10
		Subtotal			789	06
		6% Sales tax			47	34
		Invoice total			836	40

Page 135

1. $88.35
2. $1,335.00
3. 44.50
   1,438.79
   71.94
   1,510.73
4. 813.57
   39,864.68
   1,793.91
   41,658.59
5. 3.5%
6. 2.5%

Page 140

	List Price	Discount Rate	Discount Amount	Net Price
1.	1,350	6 %	81	1269.00
2.	897	10.65 %	95.50	801.50
3.	1,551	6.23 %	96.70	1454.30
4.	746.88	12 %	89.63	657.25
5.	2,360	15.32 %	361.60	1,998.40
6.	995	8 %	79.60	915.40
7.	1,675	3 1/2 %	58.63	1616.37
8.	4,168	3 1/3 %	138.79	4029.21
9.	2,780	4 %	111.20	2668.80
10.	4344.83	13 %	564.83	3,780

Page 142

1. 13.29
   25.25
   34.09
2. 26.53
   35.25
   38.07
3. 59.97
   64.77
   66.49
4. 34.41
   78.46
   86.30
5. 35.97
   68.35
   123.02
6. 88.86
   231.92
   141.95
7. 100.13
   90.11
   81.10

252.51
227.26
193.17
352.47
317.22
279.15
539.73
474.96
408.47
653.81
575.35
489.05
683.46
615.11
492.09
799.73
567.81
425.86
901.12
811.01
729.91

Page 143

8. 83.70
   77.84
   103.42
9. 354.14
   301.02
   255.87
10. 139.65
    185.54
    250.47
11. 83.79
    191.04
    252.17
12. 5,318.28
13. 17,681.88
14 57.11
15. 588.40
16. 4,076.82

1,111.99
1,034.15
930.73
2,006.81
1,705.79
1,449.92
1,855.35
1,669.81
1,419.34
1,592.01
1,400.97
1,148.80

Page 144

1. 890
2. 2994
3. 2130
4. 1971
5. 219,445
6. 272,671
7. 153,394
8. 172,524
9. 14,555
10. 1,094
11. 15,219
12. 36,568
13. 223,178
14. −19,312
15. 550,527
16. −181,744
17. 1,379
18. 893
19. 1,641
20. 2,861
21. 3,621
22. 27,154
23. 1,133.89
24. 1,821.24
25. 868.73
26. 1,451.75
27. 1,781.12
28. 2,277.40
29. 1,364.78
30. 2,128.00

Page 145

Discount

1. $00.00
2. 16.52
3. 12.80
4. 21.29
5. 50.00

Total

1. $3,500.00
2. 809.23
3. 307.08
4. 688.24
5. 4,950.00

**Invoice
Number:** 15494

Gifts Inc.

4782 E. Event Lane

Gift City, USA 00344

CUSTOMER ORDER NO.	SALESMAN	TERMS		INVOICE PAID IN:	F.O.B.	DATE
69815	Jason	20% Discount to Trade 3/10, 2/20, N/30		17 Days	—	4/3

ITEM	QUANTITY	DESCRIPTION	UNIT PRICE		AMOUNT	
4994	700	Candles		29	203	00
2001	49	Candle holders	3	00	147	00
0088	150	Calendars		50	75	00
6733	60	Pen sets	1	55	93	00
5987	65	Plaques	2	00	130	00
0027	224	U.S.A. maps		19	42	56
1266	80	Ashtrays		90	72	00
		Subtotal			756	56
		Trade discount			152	51
		Subtotal			610	05
		Purchase discount			12	20
		Invoice total			597	85

57

	List price	Discount Rate	Discount Amount	Net Price
7.	$4,700	8%	$376.00	$4,324
8.	$5,500	7.5%	$412.50	$5,087.50
9.	$4,040	5%	$202	$3,838.00
10.	$3,108	15%	$466	$2,642.00
11.	$9,500	80%	$7,600	$1,900

Invoice
Number: 15494

Corner Drug Store Inc.

2322 Avenue B

Anywhere, USA 00562

CUSTOMER ORDER NO.	SALESMAN	TERMS	INVOICE PAID IN:	F.O.B.	DATE
86-7201	John	25% Discount to Trade 3/15, 2/30, N/60	60 Days	—	4/4

ITEM	QUANTITY	DESCRIPTION	UNIT PRICE		AMOUNT	
0031	30	Lawn chairs	5	20	156	00
0492	70	Iced tea glasses		75	52	50
9802	120	#100 Film	1	50	180	00
2377	90	Cassette tapes		80	72	00
4621	170	Nail clipper sets		60	102	00
0183	45	Sunglasses (Pairs)	2	09	94	05
4707	24	Watchbands	1	75	42	00
6200	48	Small ice chests		98	47	04
		Subtotal			745	59
		Trade discount			186	40
		Subtotal			559	19
		Purchase discount			00	00
		Invoice total			559	19

	Discount		Total
1.	$145.50	**1.**	$4,704.50
2.	11.00	**2.**	539.00
3.	14.72	**3.**	721.37
4.	$1,899.36	**4.**	7,597.44
	1,139.62		6,457.82
	710.36		5,747.46
5.	$753.69	**5.**	5,527.08
	663.25		4,863.83
	729.57		4,134.26

Page 148

List price	Discount Rate	Discount Amount	Net Price
1. $8,000	15%	_$1200.00_	_$6800_
2. $6,400	_10%_	$640.00	$5,760
3. _$809_	17%	$137.53	_$671.47_

4. List price 10,350.00

First discount   _10_ % _1035_   Net price 9,315
Second discount _10_ % _932_   Net price 8,383
Third discount _10_ % _838_   Net price 7,545

5. List price 24,955.28

First discount   _7.50_ % _1,872.28_ Net price 23,083
Second discount 15 % _3,462.45_ Net price _19,620.55_
Third discount _15.44_ % 3,029   Net price _16,591.55_

Page 151

1. _____ $7.50 _____
2. _____ 61.25 _____
3. _____ 190.74 _____
4. _____ 131.94 _____
5. _____ 373.84 _____
6. _____ 333.25 _____
7. _____ 187.27 _____
8. _____ 315.61 _____

	Markup	Selling Price
1.	$543.60	$1,751.60
2.	1,283.30	4,573.80
3.	1,013.46	3,909.06
4.	1,824.34	6,385.20
5.	1,672.00	5,472.00
6.	1,824.46	6,625.66
7.	3,156.12	11,046.42

1.	$67.50
2.	110.76
3.	696.00
4.	931.50
5.	282.24

Page 154

	Markup	Percent
1.	16.56	35.78
2.	19.15	32.21
3.	18.82	24.95
4.	12.64	14.67
5.	7.22	7.90
6.	22.02	17.21
7.	97.57	82.81
8.	160.90	97.95
9.	131.16	41.15
10.	264.27	38.79

Page 156

	Markup	Percent
1.	20.00	11.77
2.	31.45	24.20
3.	79.45	41.94
4.	104.37	19.72
5.	259.68	27.36
6.	419.19	30.22
7.	629.98	33.17
8.	100.80	6.63
9.	139.08	7.80
10.	430.35	15.10

	Markup	Percent
1.	972.80	94.85
2.	170.41	11.40
3.	860.00	51.19
4.	4,040.64	116.23
5.	8,597.36	81.96
6.	6,074.63	25.67
7.	1,904.72	15.88
8.	2,686.37	17.03
9.	11,537.77	31.56
10.	1,560.00	9.48
11.	1,148.50	14.54
12.	(1,884.97)	(34.94)

	Cost	Retail Price	Markup	Markup Rate (%)
1.	$4,000	$5,000	$1,000	25%
2.	$6,600	$9,240	$ 2,640	40%
3.	$3,250	$3,737.50	$487.50	15%
4.	$384	$495	$111.00	28.91%
5.	$275.10	$371.39	$96.29	35%
6.	$2,350.60	$3,400	$1,049.40	44.64%
7.	$3,435.56	$4,270.80	$835.24	24.31%
8.	$1,926.24	$2,475.22	$548.98	28.5%
9.	$389.01	$635.26	$246.25	63.30%
10.	$1,436.96	$2,348.21	$911.25	63.42%

	Cost	Retail Price	Markup	Markup Rate (%)
1.	$10,500	$12,000	$1,500	12.5%
2.	$890	$1,090	$200	18.35%
3.	$11,780	$15,500	$3,720	24%
4.	$7,270	$9,670	$2,400	24.82%
5.	$23,680	$27,990	$4,310	15.40%
6.	$484.32	$750.88	$266.56	35.5%
7.	$1,246.75	$1,745.25	$498.50	28.56%
8.	$2,506.20	$3,676.25	$1,170.05	31.83%
9.	$780.64	$880.64	$100.00	11.36%
10.	$3,221.84	$ 5,498.02	$2,276.18	41.4%

Revenue and Expenses by Division (amounts in thousands)

	East	Midwest	West	South	Total	Average
Rev: Rental	617	701	329	1,234	2881	720.3
Moving	1,245	987	550	703	3485	871.3
Total Rev.	1862	1688	879	1937	6366	1591.5
% Revenue	29.2%	26.5%	13.8%	30.4%		
Exp: Salaries	826	739	460	237	2262	565.5
Upkeep	321	299	203	561	1384	346
Car Impr.	250	167	94	329	840	210
Total Exp.	1397	1205	757	1127	4486	1121.5
Profit	465	483	122	810	1880	470
% Profit	24.7%	25.7%	6.5%	43.1%		

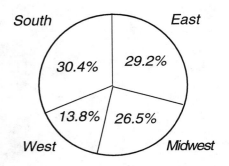

Figure 14.2. Revenues by division

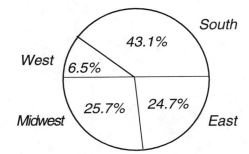

Figure 14.3. Profits by division

Revenue and Expenses by Quarter (amounts in thousands)

	First	Second	Third	Fourth	Total	Average
Rev: Rental	437	578	751	563	2329	582.3
Moving	987	621	1,207	825	3640	910
Total Rev.	1424	1199	1958	1388	5969	1492.3
% Revenue	23.9%	20.1%	32.8%	23.3%		
Exp: Salaries	204	198	235	291	928	232
Upkeep	75	68	71	95	309	77.3
Car Impr.	221	201	198	220	840	210
Total Exp.	500	467	504	606	2077	519.3
Profit	924	732	1454	782	3892	973
% Profit	23.7%	18.8%	37.4%	20.1%		

Page 167

1.	$150,000
2.	250,000
3.	1,350,000
4.	11.1%
5.	5,000
6.	25,000
7.	20,000
8.	0
9.	55.6%
10.	12.5%

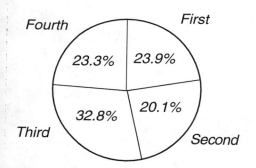

Figure 14.4.   Revenue by quarter

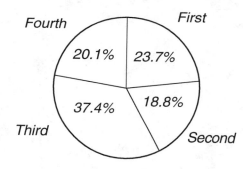

Figure 14.4.   Profit by quarter

Revenue by Quarter (amounts in thousands)

	First	Second	Third	Fourth	Total	Average
1. Rev: Books	19	26	22	30	97	24.3
2. Mag.	25	21	26	21	93	23.3
3. Newsp.	36	37	35	36	144	36
4. Total Rev.	80	84	83	87	334	83.5
5. % Revenue	24.0%	25.1%	24.9%	26.0%		

Profit by Quarter (amounts in thousands)

	First	Second	Third	Fourth	Total	Average
6. Profit: Books	3.4	4.9	4.1	7.0	19.4	4.9
7. Mag.	4.2	3.2	4.7	3.5	15.6	3.9
8. Newsp.	5.1	5.2	5.0	5.1	20.4	5.1
9. Total Profit	12.7	13.3	13.8	15.6	55.4	13.9
10. % Profit	22.9%	24.0%	24.9%	28.2%		

1. % revenue by division:

A = <u>$65,120</u>   B = <u>$45,760</u>
C = <u>21,120</u>   D = <u>44,000</u>

2. Find the profit by division based on the following percents of revenue by division. That is, percent profit = profit ÷ revenue.

A (15.5%) <u>$10,093.60</u>   B (22.7%) <u>$10,387.52</u>
C (28.1%) <u>5,934.72</u>   D (8.5%) <u>3,740.00</u>

3. Partition the circle to form a graph showing profits by division.

Profits by Division

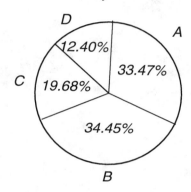

Figure 14.10   Pie chart 2

Revenue by Quarter (amounts in thousands)

		First	Second	Third	Fourth	Total	Average
Rev:	Div. A	3.6	4.2	1.8	6.6	16.2	4.05
	Div. B	7.1	6.5	8.1	3.8	25.5	6.38
	Div. C	10.1	12.3	9.2	10.5	42.1	10.53
Total Rev.		20.8	23.0	19.1	20.9	83.8	20.95
% Revenue		24.8%	27.4%	22.8%	24.9%		

1. Find the overtime rate for each at 1.5 times the regular rate.

2. At 40 hours for regular pay, find hours for regular and overtime pay.

Regular Rate	Overtime Rate	Total Hours	Regular Pay	Overtime
$7.00	_$10.50_	47	_$280.00_	_$73.50_
$6.84	_10.26_	38	_259.92_	_0.00_
$9.73	_14.60_	52	_389.20_	_175.20_

Total Gross Wages Summary

Employee Name	Hours	Rate/ Hour Regular Time	Total Over-time Hours	Over-time Rate/ Hour	Wages for Regular Hours	Wages for Over-time Hours	Total Wages
3. Berge, G.	45	7.50	_5_	$11.15	$300.00	$56.25	$356.25
4. Doe, J.	38	10.50	_0_	_15.75_	_399.00_	_0.00_	_399.00_
5. Ellis, M.	37	15.75	_0_	_23.63_	_582.75_	_0.00_	_582.75_
6. Jones, J.	52	21.80	_12_	_32.70_	_872.00_	_392.40_	_1264.40_
Total	172		_17_		_2153.75_	_448.65_	_2602.40_

Total Gross Wages Summary

Employee Name	Hours	Rate/ Hour Regular Time	Total Over-time Hours	Over-time Rate/ Hour	Wages for Regular Hours	Wages for Over-time Hours	Total Wages
7. Donovan, B.	42	22.75	_2_	$34.13	$910.00	$68.26	$978.26
8. Roe, B.	43	18.60	_3_	_27.90_	_744.00_	_83.70_	_827.70_
9. Johnson, S.	35	16.25	_0_	_24.38_	_568.75_	_0.00_	_568.75_
10. McNeil, R.	51	15.50	_11_	_23.25_	_620.00_	_255.75_	_875.75_
Total	_171_		_16_		_2842.75_	_407.71_	_3250.46_

Page 175

Name	Gross Wages	Federal Tax	Insurance 2.6%	State Tax 3.25%	FICA 7.65%	Net Pay
1. Ashe	317	29.71	$8.24	$10.30	$24.25	$244.50
2. Best	488.20	37.61	12.69	15.87	37.35	384.68
3. Clark	506.14	42.08	13.16	16.45	38.72	395.73
4. Dinzo	248.70	23.07	6.47	8.08	19.03	192.05
5. Ernst	403.56	35.17	10.49	13.12	30.87	313.91
6. Gold	311.84	25.90	8.11	10.13	23.86	243.84
7. Holz	529.41	19.53	13.76	17.21	40.50	438.41
8. Kelly	365.18	20.55	9.49	11.87	27.94	295.33
9. Luis	498.37	26.59	12.96	16.20	38.13	404.49
10. Mot	410.42	31.87	10.67	13.34	31.40	323.14

Page 176

1. 2220
2. 2220
3. 2748
4. 2454
5. 182,322
6. 272,368
7. 219,973
8. 181,520
9. 28,093
10. 15,862
11. 11,198
12. 52,190
13. −203,010
14. 601,999
15. 39,870
16. 51,289
17. 214,858
18. 6,020
19. 2,772
20. 10,650
21. 26,877
22. 32,700
23. 1,206.01
24. 1,756.46
25. 826.44
26. 1,376.26
27. 1,891.65
28. 1,644.33
29. 1,983.58
30. 1,184.21

Total Gross Wages Summary

Employee Name	Total Hours	Rate/ Hour Regular Time	Total Over- time Hours	Over- time Rate/ Hour	Wages for Regular Hours	Wages for Over- time Hours	Total Wages
A. Grindy, L.	42	24.25	2	$36.38	$970.00	$72.76	$1042.76
B. Vacario, V.	46	14.50	6	21.75	580.00	130.50	710.50
C. Waters, B.	49	19.60	9	29.40	784.00	264.60	1048.60
D. Kumler, R.	39	21.80	0	32.70	850.20	0.00	850.20
E. Weinstein, G.	40	23.80	0	35.70	952.00	0.00	952.00
Total	216		17	155.93	4136.20	467.86	4604.06

Deductions and Net Pay Summary

Employee Name	Gross Wages	Federal Income Taxes	Insurance 5.5%	State Tax 6.1%	Retire- ment 6%	FICA 7.1%	Net Pay
A. Grindy, L.		85.20	$57.35	$63.61	$62.57	$74.04	$699.99
B. Vacario, V.		57.46	39.08	43.34	42.63	50.45	477.54
C. Waters, B.		61.44	57.67	63.96	62.92	74.45	728.16
D. Kumler, R.		78.35	46.76	51.86	51.01	60.36	561.86
E. Weinstein, G.		81.50	52.36	58.07	57.12	67.59	635.36
Total	216	363.95	253.22	280.84	276.25	326.89	3102.91

(total gross wages: $4604.06)

73

Total Gross Wages Summary

Employee Name	Total Hours	Rate/ Hour Regular Time	Total Over-time Hours	Over-time Rate/ Hour	Wages for Regular Hours	Wages for Over-time Hours	Total Wages
K. Hatch	48	14.25	8	$21.38	$570.00	$171.04	$741.04
A. Irace	39	18.75	0	28.13	731.25	0.00	731.25
P. Krom	47	19.60	7	29.40	784.00	205.80	989.80
C. Mendez	40	15.20	0	22.80	608.00	0.00	608.00
N. Nole	40	8.50	0	12.75	340.00	0.00	340.00
Total	214	76.30	15	114.46	3033.25	376.84	3410.09

Deductions and Net Pay Summary

Employee Name	Gross Wages	Federal Income Taxes	Insurance 5.5%	State Tax 6.1%	Retire-ment 6%	FICA 7.1%	Net Pay
K. Hatch	$741.04	64.28	$40.76	$45.20	$44.46	$52.61	$493.73
A. Irace	731.25	56.09	40.22	44.61	43.88	51.92	494.53
P. Krom	989.80	72.13	54.44	60.38	59.39	70.28	673.18
C. Mendez	608.00	48.72	33.44	37.09	36.48	43.17	409.10
N. Nole	340.00	31.65	18.70	20.74	20.40	24.14	224.37
Total	3410.09	272.87	187.56	208.02	204.61	242.12	2294.91

	This Year	Last Year	Increase/ Decrease	Percent
1.	$1,690.00	$2,380.00	$(690.00)	(28.99)%
2.	$3,150.00	$2,990.36	$ 159.64	5.34 %
3.	$3,862.00	$4,650.25	$(788.25)	(16.95)%
4.	$6,895.40	$5,906.00	$ 989.40	16.75 %
5.	$8,535.06	$9,176.61	$(641.55)	(6.99) %
6.	$12,334.45	$10,998.47	$1335.98	12.15 %
7.	$17,452.83	$19,246.35	$(1,793.52)	(9.32) %
8.	$22,350.35	$21,987.66	$ 362.69	1.65 %
9.	$88,461.19	$87,968.23	$ 492.96	.56 %
10.	$49,540.00	$48,539.75	$1,000.25	2.06 %
11.	$62,170.49	$64,480.00	$(2,309.51)	(3.58) %
12.	$71,380.00	$91,572.30	$(20,192.30)	(22.05) %
13.	$168,291.35	$159,360.00	$ 8,931.35	5.60 %
14.	$129,303.66	$141,060.35	$(11,756.69)	(8.33) %
15.	$155,110.00	$149,209.41	$ 5,900.59	3.95 %
16.	$69,850.00	$46,800.75	$ 23,049.25	49.25 %

	This Year	Last Year	Increase/ Decrease	Percent
17.	$34,775.00	$ 25,800.00	$8,975.00	34.79 %
18.	$ 28,415.35	$18,065.35	$10,350.00	57.29 %
19.	$25,380.45	$ 23,730.45	$1,650.00	6.95 %
20.	$ 49,493.66	$ 38,528.46	$10,965.20	28.46%
21.	$14,500.00	$16,100.00	$ (1600.00)	(9.94)%
22.	$72,652.00	$ 81,779.50	$(9,127.50)	(11.16)%
23.	$52,784.60	$ 60,256.39	$ (7,471.79)	(12.4%)
24.	$19,691.00	$ 18,490.00	$1,201.00	6.50 %
25.	$ 94,113.44	$ 103,763.44	$9,650.00	(9.3%)

1. | Department | Sales for Quarter | Percent of Total |
    |---|---|---|
    | A | $ 10,350 | 3.11 |
    | B | 19,808 | 5.95 |
    | C | 26,225 | 7.87 |
    | D | 46,030 | 13.82 |
    | E | 89,450 | 26.85 |
    | F | 120,300 | 36.11 |
    | G | 20,950 | 6.29 |
    | TOTAL | $ 333,113 | 100.00 |

2. | Department | Sales for Quarter | Percent of Total |
    |---|---|---|
    | A | $ 135,000 | 24.41 |
    | B | 10,280 | 1.86 |
    | C | 46,350 | 8.38 |
    | D | 20,080 | 3.63 |
    | E | 98,360 | 17.79 |
    | F | 110,200 | 19.93 |
    | G | 67,020 | 12.12 |
    | H | 19,670 | 3.56 |
    | I | 46,086 | 8.33 |
    | TOTAL | $ 553,046 | 100.01 |

3. | Department | Sales for Quarter | Percent of Total |
    |---|---|---|
    | A | $ 498 | .28 |
    | B | 69,225 | 39.05 |
    | C | 3,627 | 2.05 |
    | D | 10,980 | 6.19 |
    | E | 1,450 | .82 |
    | F | 9,275 | 5.23 |
    | G | 7,080 | 3.99 |
    | H | 14,260 | 8.04 |
    | I | 24,388 | 13.76 |
    | J | 36,490 | 20.58 |
    | TOTAL | $ 177,273 | 99.99 |

1. Valu Company has four owners. How much of the total profits will each receive according to the percent of ownership?

Owner	Percent	Amount of Profits
Baker	40%	$26,160.00
Golden	22%	$14,388.00
Clancy	9%	$5,886.00
Wu	29%	$18,966.00
Total	100%	$65,400

2. Charges for utilities are prorated by department according to the given percents. Find the amount to be paid by each department in each category. Find answers to the nearest dollar.

Department	Percent	Heat	Electricity	Maintenance
A	36%	$1576	$1390	$2618
B	28%	1226	1081	2036
C	17%	744	656	1236
D	12%	525	463	873
E	7%	306	270	509
Total	100%	$4,378	$3,860	$7,271

1. Total expenses: $3,490

Department	Sales	Share of Expenses
A	$9,860	$442.90
B	15,340	689.06
C	23,100	1037.63
D	13,725	616.52
E	11,490	516.12
F	4,180	187.76
Total	$77,695	$3,489.99

2. Total expenses: $19,360

Department	Sales	Share of Expenses
A	$10,350	$ 601.53
B	19,808	1151.21
C	26,225	1524.16
D	46,030	2675.19
E	89,450	5198.70
F	120,300	6991.65
G	20,950	1217.58
Total	$ 333,113	$19,360.01

3. Total expenses: $23,490

Department	Sales	Share of Expenses
A	$135,000	$6255.23
B	10,280	476.32
C	46,350	2147.63
D	20,080	930.41
E	98,360	4557.51
F	110,200	5106.12
G	67,020	3105.37
H	19,670	911.41
Total	$ 506,960	$23,490.00

4. Total expenses: $7,650

Department	Sales	Share of Expenses
A	$69,225	$4549.78
B	498	32.73
C	3,627	238.38
D	10,980	721.65
E	1,450	95.30
F	9,275	609.59
G	7,080	465.33
H	14,260	937.23
Total	$ 116,395	$7649.99

	This Year	Last Year	Increase/ (Decrease)	% Increase/ (Decrease)
1.	$12,300	$11,100	*$1200*	*10.81*
2.	$15,600	$17,600	*(2000)*	*11.36*
3.	$19,460	*$17,270*	$2,190	*12.68*
4.	$50,210	*$53,470*	($3,260)	*6.10*
5.	*$28,030*	$23,740	$4,290	*18.07*

Allocate expenses of $7,620 proportionately to sales of the departments.

	Department	Sales	Expenses
6.	A	$7,420	*$2185.56*
7.	B	2,140	*630.34*
8.	C	4,980	*1466.86*
9.	D	10,410	*3066.26*
10.	E	920	*270.99*
11.	Total	*25,870*	*7620.01*

	This Year	Last Year	Increase/ (Decrease)	% Increase/ (Decrease)
1.	$41,000	$45,000	*($4000)*	*(8.89%)*
2.	$31,250	$28,910	*$2,340*	*8.09%*
3.	$37,600	*$42,190*	($4,590)	*(10.88%)*
4.	$98,020	*$88,150*	$ 9,870	*11.20%*
5.	*$20,084.04*	$23,740	*($3655.96)*	(15.4%)

Allocate expenses of $67,500 proportionately to sales of the departments. Calculate the percent of expenses allocated to each department.

	Department	Sales	Expenses	% Expenses
6.	A	$65,030	*$34,881.79*	*51.68*
7.	B	8,760	*4698.82*	*6.96*
8.	C	28,400	*15,233.63*	*22.57*
9.	D	17,300	*9279.64*	*13.75*
10.	E	6,350	*3406.11*	*5.05*
11.	Total	*$125,840*	*$67,499.99*	*100.01*

Department	Sales	Quota	Dollar Difference	Percent Over/Under Quota
A	$ 9,860	$ 9,500	$ _360.00_	_3.79_
B	15,340	15,800	_(460.00)_	_(2.91)_
C	23,100	24,500	_(1400.00)_	_(5.71)_
D	13,725	12,500	_1225.00_	_9.80_
E	4,180	2,775	_1405.00_	_50.63_
Total	$ _66,205_	$ _65,075_	$ _1130.00_	_1.74_

Calculate the following:

Department	Sales	Quota	Dollar Difference	Percent Over/Under Quota
A	$ 10,350	$ 9,675	$ _675.00_	_6.98_
B	19,808	21,300	_(1492.00)_	_(7.00)_
C	26,225	27,900	_(1675.00)_	_(6.00)_
D	46,030	45,000	_1030.00_	_2.29_
E	89,450	70,000	_19,450.00_	_27.79_
F	120,300	136,985	_(16,685.00)_	_(12.18)_
G	20,950	27,500	_(6550.00)_	_(23.82)_
Total	$_333,113_	$_338,360_	$_(5247.00)_	_(1.55)_

Department	Sales	Quota	Dollar Difference	Percent Over/Under Quota
A	$135,000	$139,000	$ (4000.00)	(2.88)
B	10,280	15,000	(4720.00)	(31.47)
C	46,350	49,500	(3150.00)	(6.36)
D	20,080	16,750	3330.00	19.88
E	98,360	105,225	(6865.00)	(6.52)
F	110,200	100,000	(10,220.00)	10.20
G	67,020	70,900	(3880.00)	(5.47)
H	19,670	21,000	(1330.00)	(6.33)
I	46,086	46,000	86.00	.19
Total	$553,046	$563,375	$(10,329.00)	(1.83)

Department	Sales	Quota	Dollar Difference	Percent Over/Under Quota
A	$ 498	$ 450	$ 48.00	10.67
B	69,225	70,000	(775.00)	(1.11)
C	3,627	3,000	627.00	20.90
D	10,980	12,225	(1245.00)	(10.18)
E	1,450	1,500	(50.00)	(3.33)
F	9,275	10,000	(725.00)	(7.25)
G	7,080	6,500	580.00	8.92
H	14,260	15,800	(1540.00)	(9.75)
I	24,388	26,390	(2002.00)	(7.59)
J	36,490	35,500	990.00	2.79
Total	$177,273	$181,365	$(4092.00)	(2.26)

1. Budget Analysis

	Year: 1992 Budget	Percent of Total Sales	Year: 1992 Actual	Percent of Total Sales	Year 1993 Proj'd.	Percent of Total Sales
Income/Sales:						
Dept-A	$1,200,000	40.68%	$1,224,000	39.50%	$1,650,000	43.14%
Dept-B	700,000	23.73%	675,000	21.78%	725,000	18.95%
Dept-C	1,050,000	35.59%	1,200,000	38.72%	1,450,000	37.91%
Total Sales:	$ 2,950,000	100%	$ 3,099,000	100%	$ 3,825,000	100%

2. Cost of Goods Sold (COGS)

	Year: 1992 Budget	Percent of Total Sales	Year: 1992 Actual	Percent of Total Sales	Year 1993 Proj'd.	Percent of Total Sales
Dept-A	$501,000	16.98%	$510,500	16.47%	$830,000	21.70%
Dept-B	425,000	14.41%	410,000	13.23%	485,000	12.68%
Dept-C	730,000	24.75%	740,000	23.88%	780,000	20.39%
Total COGS:	$ 1,656,000	100%	$ 1,660,500	100%	$ 2,095,000	100%
Gross Profit:	$ 1,294,000	43.86%	$ 1,438,500	46.42%	$ 1,730,000	45.23%

Page 197

Dept.	1992 Budget	1992 Actual	Dollar Difference	% Over/ Under		1993 Projected	% Increase/ Decrease	
A	$1,200	$1,224	$ _24.00_	_2.00_	%	$1,650	_34.80_	%
B	700	675	_(25.00)_	_(3.57)_	%	725	_7.41_	%
C	1,050	1,200	_150.00_	_14.29_	%	1,450	_20.83_	%
Total Sales	$ _2950_	$ _3099_	$ _149.00_	_5.05_	%	$ _3825_	_23.43_	%

Prorating of Operating Expenses
for 1993 Projected Budget
Based on Gross Sales per Department

	1993 Proj.	Dept. A 43%	Dept. B 19%	Dept. C 38%
Operating Expenses:				
Wages/Salaries	585	$ _251,550_	$ _111,150_	$ _222,300_
Executive Salaries	295	$ _126,850_	$ _56,050_	$ _112,100_
Rent	155	$ _66,650_	$ _29,450_	$ _58,900_
Utilities	120.5	$ _51,815_	$ _22,895_	$ _45,790_
Insurance	56.5	$ _24,295_	$ _10,735_	$ _21,470_
Office Supplies	37.3	$ _16,039_	$ _7,087_	$ _14,174_
Sales Commissions	285	$ _122,550_	$ _54,150_	$ _108,300_
Entertainment	12.5	$ _5,375_	$ _2,375_	$ _4,750_
Total Operating (Expenses)	_1,546,800_	$ _665,124_	$ _293,892_	$ _587,784_

Page 198

1. _2,220_
2. _2,850_
3. _1,878_
4. _1,936_
5. _336,180_
6. _97,111_
7. _209,610_
8. _178,296_
9. _48,144_
10. _62,809_
11. _78,488_
12. _−7,141_
13. _−92,258_
14. _799,620_
15. _50,395_
16. _279,476_
17. _7,176_
18. _9,996_
19. _8,235_
20. _28,875_
21. _9,030_
22. _12,120_
23. _1,173.10_
24. _1,604.00_
25. _1,140.19_
26. _1,467.68_
27. _1,470.70_
28. _2,244.12_
29. _1,090.16_
30. _1,726.71_

1.

OPERATING EXPENSES

	Year: 1992 Budget	Percent of Total Sales	Year: 1992 Actual	Percent of Total Sales	Year 1993 Proj'd.	Percent of Total Sales
Wages/ Salaries	$ 460,750	15.62 %	$ 456,400	14.73 %	$ 585,000	15.29 %
Executive Salary	235,554	7.98 %	242,500	7.83 %	295,000	7.71 %
Rent	131,664	4.46 %	131,664	4.25 %	155,000	4.05 %
Utilities	97,725	3.31 %	107,000	3.45 %	120,500	3.15 %
Insurance	37,878	1.28 %	48,500	1.57 %	56,480	1.48 %
Office Supplies	29,950	1.02 %	34,650	1.12 %	37,300	0.98 %
Sales Com- missions	195,000	6.61 %	216,000	6.97 %	285,000	7.45 %
Entertainment	8,429	0.29 %	10,380	0.33 %	12,500	0.33 %
Total Operating Expenses	$ 1,196,950	40.57 %	$1,247,094	40.24 %	$ 1,546,780	40.44 %
Profit	$ 97,050	3.29 %	$191,406	6.18 %	$ 253,220	6.62 %

2. Cost of Goods Sold.

3. $50,144

4. 4.19%

Department	Sales	Quota	Dollar Difference	Percent Over/Under Quota
A	$ 5,380	$ 4915	$ 465	9.46
B	13,504	15,820	(2316)	(14.64)
C	4063	4,926	(863)	(17.52)
D	22,010	20,630	1,380	6.69
E	11,637	16,444	(4,807)	(29.23)
F	8385	8,360	25	.30
G	29,322.81	19,832.81	9,490	47.85
H	9,275	7,100	2175	30.63
I	7245	6,350	895	14.09
J	14,080	16,380	(2,300)	(14.04)
K	29,957.98	25,637.98	4,320	16.85
Total	$ 154,859.79	$ 146,395.79	$ 8464	5.78

Page 201

	1992 Expenses	1993 Prorated Expenses	Percent
Operating Expenses:			
Wages/Salaries	$ 28.5	$ 25,846.92	40.2 %
Executive Salaries	$ 12.1	$ 10,973.62	17.1 %
Rent	$ 5.2	$ 4,715.94	7.3 %
Utilities	$ 4.7	$ 4,262.48	6.6 %
Insurance	$ 3.2	$ 2,902.12	4.5 %
Office Supplies	$ 2.5	$ 2,267.28	3.5 %
Sales Commissions	$ 10.4	$ 9,431.88	14.7 %
Entertainment	$ 4.3	$ 3,899.72	6.1 %
Total Operating Expenses	$ 70.9	$ 64,300	100 %

Page 205

Interest	Total to be Repaid
1. $10.00	1. $110.00
2. 65.00	2. 565.00
3. 30.00	3. 280.00
4. 140.40	4. 1700.40
5. 74.34	5. 782.34

Page 207

1. $912.00
2. 1,090.20
3. 360.75
4. 717.19
5. 1,209.00
6. 28.00
7. 158.70

Interest	Repayment
1. $38.50	1. $588.50
2. 264.00	2. 1,464.00
3. 1,055.25	3. 4,405.25
4. 1,840.63	4. 7,730.63
5. 148.44	5. 3,273.44
3,000.00	9,000.00
2,380.00	10,880.00
1,197.50	5,987.50

Page 208

Interest

1.	$664.63	1.	*$14.63*
2.	963.83	2.	*$28.83*
3.	1,083.37	3.	*$56.88*
4.	1,283.90	4.	*$58.10*
5.	2,158.46	5.	*$172.15*
6.	2,578.16	6.	*$84.49*
7.	3,817.48	7.	*$317.48*
8.	5,564.50	8.	*$414.50*
9.	6,613.40	9.	*$383.40*
10.	9,321.38	10.	*$884.26*
11.	10,074.24	11.	*$393.29*
12.	7,283.19	12.	*$200.19*
13.	1,640.10	13.	*$100.10*
14.	870.88	14.	*$8.39*
15.	513.13	15.	*$13.13*

Page 209

	Interest	=	Principal	x	Rate	x	Time (Years)
1.	$1,100		$5,000		*11%*		2
2.	$712.50		$3,000		9.5%		*2.5*
3.	$586.50		$*5,100*		11.5%		*1*
4.	$*409.76*		$2,230		12.25%		1.5
5.	$690		$*3,450*		8%		2.5
6.	$136.90		$740		18.5%		*1*
7.	$15,962.50		$25,000		*12.77%*		5
8.	$1,050		$20,000		*10.5%*		0.5
9.	$*4368*		$11,200		6.5%		6
10.	$3,403.125		$16,500		*8.25%*		2.5

	Interest	=	Principal	x	Rate	x	Time (Years)
1.	$348.00		$2,900		6%		2
2.	1225.50		$4,300		9.5%		3
3.	169.28		$915		18.5%		1
4.	1429.75		$3,800		10.75%		3.5
5.	4081.00		$7,700		13.25%		4

	Interest	=	Principal	x	Rate	x	Time (Days)
6.	$468.05		$12,210		11.5%		120
7.	63.80		$1,760		14.5%		90
8.	76.44		$728		21%		180
9.	58.88		$516.98		20.5%		200
10.	3035.36		$21,876.45		18.5%		270

Page 211

	Interest =	Principal x	Rate x	Time (Years)
1.	$648	*$2700*	12%	2
2.	$354.38	$1,350	*10.5%*	2.5
3.	*$617.50*	$1,900	6.5%	5
4.	$6,440	$14,000	11.5%	*4*
5.	$351.90	$782	*18%*	2.5
6.	$5,512.50	$ 9,000	12.25%	*5*
7.	$596.63	*$1850.02*	21.5%	1.5
8.	*$1500.56*	$3,775	13.25%	3
9.	$138.74	$562	*19.75%*	1.25
10.	$713.36	*$1281.01*	20.25	2.75

Page 215

1. 9,765,625.0000
2. 12,230.5905
3. 8,279.2891
4. 9.6684
5. 1,801.1527
6. 1.8114
7. 2.9589
8. 14,539.3357
9. 1.7908
10. 1.7081
11. $136.05
12. 1,770.14
13. 998.59
14. 2,679.73
15. 2,719.42
16. 18,376.63
17. 201.16
18. 2,005.77
19. 12,889.02
20. 6,005.07
21. 20,121.96
22. 14,105.19
23. 15,325.27
24. 404.64
25. 3,218.50

Page 217

1. $2,367.36
2. 13,129.96
3. 26,573.42
4. 79,328.52
5. 77,221.81
6. 322,553.25
7. 142,136.95
8. 323,132.76
9. 5,187,484.00
10. 21,253,963.92

Page 218

1. 16 years
2. 8 years
3. 10 years
4. 7 years
5. 9 years
6. 5 years
7. multiplied by 4
8. multiplied by 9
9. 10%
10. 11%
11. $4720.57

Page 219

1. 282,475,249.00
2. 13,723.10
3. 1.70
4. 6.02
5. $1593.25
6. 3379.44
7. 10,894.80
8. 13,477.14
9. 7.2%
10. 5.3%

Page 220

1. $1297.38
2. 8257.28
3. 24,059.96
4. 2538.61
5. 9 years
6. 7 years
7. 6 years
8. 13 years
9. 7.4%
10. 20.2%

Page 223

1. $90.00
2. 240.00
3. 532.00
4. 1,925.00
5. 1,162.53
6. 1,070.65
7. 114.19
8. 37.69
9. 9.56
10. 247.00

Page 224

1. $50.00
Interest Amount
45.83
Monthly Payment
2. 275.00
Interest Amount
63.54
Monthly Payment
3. 718.75
Interest Amount
107.29
Monthly Payment
4. 1546.13
Interest Amount
147.53
Monthly Payment
5. 95.09
Interest Amount
66.01
Monthly Payment
6. 269.33
Interest Amount
77.97
Monthly Payment
7. 530.40
Interest Amount
76.61
Monthly Payment
8. 2646.00
Interest Amount
205.86
Monthly Payment
9. 21.72
Interest Amount
87.79
Monthly Payment
10. 32.56
Interest Amount
50.67
Monthly Payment

Page 225

1. $45.00
Interest Amount
45.42
Monthly Payment
16.62%
Annual Interest Rate
2. $84.38
Interest Amount
50.63
Monthly Payment
18.75%
Annual Interest Rate
3. $140.25
Interest Amount
55.01
Monthly Payment
20.84%
Annual Interest Rate
4. $180.00
Interest Amount
49.17
Monthly Payment
17.28%
Annual Interest Rate
5. $300.00
Interest Amount
60.00
Monthly Payment
15.48%
Annual Interest Rate
6. $157.50
Interest Amount
107.68
Monthly Payment
18.67%
Annual Interest Rate

Page 227

1. $440.40
2. 430.00
3. 151,200.00
4. 166,518.00
5. 54,000
6. 283,500.00

Page 228

1. $2128.00
2. $65.00
3. $638.25
4. $157.17
5. 19.2%
6. 33.23%
7. $126.67
8. $61.45
9. 22.74%
10. 39.38%

Principal	Rate	Number of Payments	Interest Amount	Monthly Payment	True Annual Interest Rate
11. $312.76	11.6%	15	$45.35	$23.87	21.75%
12. $785.01	20.5%	27	362.09	42.49	39.54%
13. $901.67	18.75%	30	422.66	44.14	36.29%
14. $478.10	15.3%	20	121.92	30.00	29.14%
15. $309.78	10.2%	12	31.60	28.45	18.83%

Page 229

1. $108.00
2. $281.40
3. $173.85
4. $531.88
5. $45.50
   32.96
6. 486.00
   76.50
7. $33.00
   25.67
   22.15%
8. $9.17
   16.77
   19.56%

Page 230

1. $161.50
2. $769.50
3. $651.00
4. $138.86
5. $73.50
   35.29
6. $644.96
   129.27
7. $1.50
   12.88
   14.40%
8. $78.00
   21.90
   24.76%

Page 233

1. 49,700
   8,400
2. 191,400
   66,900
3. 414,489
   46,889
4. 210,000
   33,700
5. 109,327
   19,159
6. 419,777
   78,737
7. 470,874
   228,984
8. 112,929
   (24,279)
9. 317,921
   150,918
10. 463,044
    176,534

Page 235

1. 46.25%
2. 21.49%
3. 67.74%
4. 18.08%
5. 49.66%
6. 50.34%
7. 28.74%
8. 2.28%
9. 1.76%
10. 2.53%
11. 1.62%
12. 36.93%
13. 13.41%

BELGO'S HOME FURNISHINGS

INCOME STATEMENT

For the Quarter Ended September 1992

		Percent of Net Sales
Revenue:		
Sales	$295,700	
Less: Returns	16,000	
Net sales	$279,700	
Cost of goods sold:		
Merchandise inventory, July 1	$108,500	**1.** 38.79%
Purchases	57,300	**2.** 20.49%
COG available for sale, July 1	$165,800	**3.** 59.28%
Less: Mdse Inv., Sept. 30 ...	39,100	**4.** 13.98%
Cost of goods sold	$126,700	**5.** 45.30%
Gross profit	153,000	**6.** 54.70%
Operating expenses:		
Salaries expense	$ 92,100	**7.** 32.93%
Supplies expense....................	6,800	**8.** 2.43%
Office expense	5,300	**9.** 1.89%
Utilities expense	8,700	**10.** 3.11%
Miscellaneous expense...........	4,200	**11.** 1.50%
Total operating expense	$117,100	**12.** 41.87%
Net income	35,900	**13.** 12.84%

1.	2,096
2.	2,514
3.	1,604
4.	2,102
5.	162,307
6.	214,477
7.	248,373
8.	174,359
9.	55,264
10.	1,876
11.	84,405
12.	54,689
13.	568,259
14.	788,303
15.	575,458
16.	232,414
17.	4,515
18.	13,815
19.	33,935
20.	11,375
21.	15,675
22.	57,630
23.	884.51
24.	2,362.05
25.	1,628.66
26.	1,148.75
27.	1,715.00
28.	2,062.31
29.	1,128.14
30.	1,924.96

BELGO'S HOME FURNISHINGS
INCOME STATEMENT
For the Year Ended December 1992

Revenue:			Percent of Net Sales
Sales	$1,138,500		
Less: Returns	70,300		
Net sales		1,068,200	
Cost of goods sold:			
Merchandise Inventory, Jan. 1	$175,200		1. 16.40%
Purchases	438,100		2. 41.01%
COG available for sale, Jan. 1		613,300	3. 57.41%
Less: Mdse Inv., Dec. 31	$95,600		4. 8.95%
Cost of goods sold		517,700	5. 48.46%
Gross profit		550,500	6. 51.54%
Operating expenses:			
Salaries expense	$403,200		7. 37.75%
Supplies expense....................	25,300		8. 2.37%
Office expense	19,200		9. 1.80%
Utilities expense	34,700		10. 3.25%
Miscellaneous expense...........	18,500		11. 1.73%
Total operating expense		500,900	12. 46.89%
Net income		49,600	13. 4.64%

1. | Revenue | 784,300 |
   | --- | --- |
   | COGS | 302,700 |
   | Gross profit | *481,600* |
   | Operating expenses | 143,900 |
   | Net income | *337,700* |

2. | Revenue | 265,400 |
   | --- | --- |
   | COGS | 187,200 |
   | Gross profit | *78,200* |
   | Operating expenses | 74,200 |
   | Net income | *4,000* |

3. | Revenue | 504,100 |
   | --- | --- |
   | COGS | 231,200 |
   | Gross profit | *272,900* |
   | Operating expenses | 176,400 |
   | Net income | *96,500* |

4. | Revenue | 439,200 |
   | --- | --- |
   | COGS | 256,500 |
   | Gross profit | *182,700* |
   | Operating expenses | 108,600 |
   | Net income | *74,100* |

THE BOOK PALACE
INCOME STATEMENT
For the Quarter Ended December 1992

			Percent of Net Sales
Revenue:			
Sales	$265,400		
Less: Returns	16,300		
Net sales		$249,100	
Cost of goods sold:			
Merchandise Inventory, Jan. 1	$31,700		1. 12.73%
Purchases	$182,400		2. 73.22%
COG available for sale, Jan. 1	$214,100		3. 85.95%
Less: Mdse Inv., Dec. 31	$24,700		4. 9.92%
Cost of goods sold		$189,400	5. 76.03%
Gross profit		$59,700	6. 23.97%

Page 243

1. _____77,900_____

Page 244

	Assets	=	Liabilities	+	Owner's Equity
1.	$67,900		$45,300		_$22,600_
2.	_$824,100_		$327,600		$496,500
3.	$761,400		_$555,300_		$206,100
4.	$952,400		$682,900		_$269,500_
5.	$204,700		$138,200		_$65,500_
6.	$1,467,200		_$1,080,000_		$387,200
7.	_$1,599,100_		$894,200		$704,900
8.	_$817,738_		$510,638		$307,100
9.	$80,200		$78,600		_$1,600_
10.	$2,674,900		_$1,591,900_		$1,083,000
11.	$612,000		$517,400		_$94,600_
12.	$198,400		_$99,300_		$99,100

Page 245

			2 000 00			11 700 00	
						23 200 00	
			34 900 00			34 900 00	

Figure 22.3   Practice balance sheet

102

1.

900	300
500	
1,400	300
Debit Balance 1,100	

2.

1,200	400
600	300
1,800	700
Debit Balance 1,100	

3.

350	75
260	
80	
690	75
Debit Balance 615	

4.

980	320
505	245
1,485	565
Debit Balance 920	

5.

1,120	316
	96
	138
1,120	550
Debit Balance 570	

6.

1,450	1529
512	
102	
2,064	1,529
Debit Balance 535	

NO. _____

DATE	EXPLANATION	POST REF.	DEBIT	CREDIT	BALANCE	
					DEBIT	CREDIT
					6540 00	
					5824 00	
					7518 00	
					7796 00	

104

_____ NO. _____

DATE		EXPLANATION	POST REF.	DEBIT	CREDIT	BALANCE	
						DEBIT	CREDIT
						8190 00	
						6001 00	
						5467 00	
						6383 00	
						6857 00	
						6445 00	

NO. _____

DATE	EXPLANATION	POST REF.	DEBIT	CREDIT	BALANCE	
					DEBIT	CREDIT
					1 1 0 0 00	
					1 4 0 7 00	
					9 5 7 00	
					1 0 4 1 00	

NO. _____

DATE		EXPLANATION	POST REF.	DEBIT	CREDIT	BALANCE	
						DEBIT	CREDIT
						1 9 6 00	
						4 6 9 00	
						5 5 0 00	
						3 5 0 00	

NO. _____

DATE		EXPLANATION	POST REF.	DEBIT	CREDIT	BALANCE	
						DEBIT	CREDIT
							2 1 0 0 00
							1 7 4 0 00
							2 2 1 9 00
							2 3 9 2 00

NO. _____

DATE		EXPLANATION	POST REF.	DEBIT	CREDIT	BALANCE			
						DEBIT		CREDIT	
								8 2 5 00	
								2 1 1 8 00	
								2 2 1 0 00	
								1 4 6 0 00	
								1 6 1 2 00	

1. _____ NO. _____

DATE	EXPLANATION	POST REF.	DEBIT	CREDIT	BALANCE	
					DEBIT	CREDIT
					1200 00	
					935 00	
					516 00	
					1220 00	

Figure 22.14   Cash account

2. _____ NO. _____

DATE	EXPLANATION	POST REF.	DEBIT	CREDIT	BALANCE	
					DEBIT	CREDIT
					534 00	
					851 00	
					956 00	
					206 00	

Figure 22.15   Accounts receivable form

3.

DATE		EXPLANATION	POST REF.	DEBIT	CREDIT	BALANCE	
						DEBIT	CREDIT
							7 95 00
							21 41 00
							14 61 00
							15 88 00
							10 98 00
							13 71 00

NO. _____

Figure 22.16   Accounts payable form

1. _____ NO. _____

DATE	EXPLANATION	POST REF.	DEBIT	CREDIT	BALANCE	
					DEBIT	CREDIT
					5 3 0 0 00	
					4 5 1 6 00	
					2 8 6 9 00	
					4 1 6 6 00	

Figure 22.17   Cash account

2. _____ NO. _____

DATE	EXPLANATION	POST REF.	DEBIT	CREDIT	BALANCE	
					DEBIT	CREDIT
					7 6 3 00	
					1 0 5 9 00	
					6 3 9 00	

Figure 22.18   Accounts receivable form

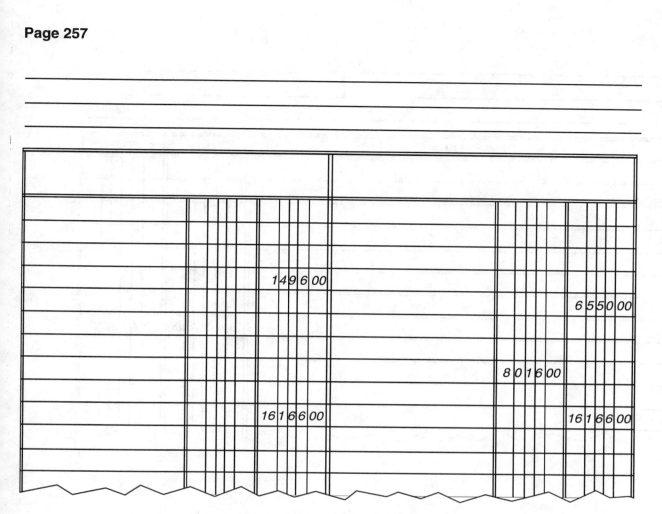

Figure 22.19   Balance sheet for Mastery Checkpoint

ACCT. NO.	ACCOUNT NAME	DEBIT	CREDIT
		3 42 00 00	3 42 00 00

ACCT. NO.	ACCOUNT NAME	DEBIT	CREDIT
		35100 00	35100 00

115

ACCT. NO.	ACCOUNT NAME	DEBIT	CREDIT
			2 1 3 0 0 00

ACCT. NO.	ACCOUNT NAME	DEBIT	CREDIT
			2320000

ACCT. NO.	ACCOUNT NAME	DEBIT	CREDIT
		1 3 6 0 0 00	
		1 4 0 0 00	
		2 9 8 0 0 00	
		1 4 0 0 00	
			2 2 6 00
			2 3 6 00
		4 6 2 0 0 00	4 6 2 0 0 00

Page 268

1. Debits = Credits
2. left
3. debit
4. liability
5. Debits

ACCT. NO.	ACCOUNT NAME	DEBIT	CREDIT
101	Cash	1 1 9 0 0 00	
102	Accounts Receivable	1 7 0 0 00	
111	Exercise Equipment	3 4 8 0 0 00	
112	Furniture	1 6 0 0 00	
201	Accounts Payable		2 6 5 0 0 00
301	Joan Li, Capital		2 3 5 0 0 00
		5 0 0 0 0 00	5 0 0 0 0 00

Answers to Tests
and
Supplemental
Touch Drills

Test 1. Lessons 1–5

1. _____ 1,866 _____
2. _____ 444 _____
3. _____ 1,101 _____
4. _____ 1,787 _____
5. _____ 1,189 _____
6. _____ 3,211 _____
7. _____ 2,521 _____
8. _____ 2,550 _____
9. _____ 3,724 _____
10. _____ 752 _____
11. _____ 26.65 _____
12. _____ 14.77 _____
13. _____ 4.67 _____
14. _____ 16.41 _____
15. _____ 15.17 _____
16. _____ 4 _____
17. _____ 22 _____
18. _____ 31 _____
19. _____ 200 _____
20. _____ 1 _____
21. _____ $124.95 _____
22. _____ $111.20 _____
23. _____ $17.85 _____
24. _____ $660.00 _____
25. _____ $914.00 _____

Test 2. Lessons 6–10

1. 45.53
2. 17.52
3. 226.40
4. 0.60
5. 0.38
6. 0.58
7. 800 mi
8. 38.5 gal
9. 20.78 mi per gal
10. 4,263
    3,251.85
    5,104.05
11. 3,503.50
    68,682.90
    436.15
12. $29.75
13. $28.98
14. $36.54
15. $23.40
16. $118.67
17. $263.21
18. bal., $586.62
19. bal., $288.58
20. bal., $288.58
21. 50%
22. 0.4
23. 40%
24. 113/100
25. 113%

NUMBER	DATE	DESCRIPTION OF TRANSACTION	PAYMENT/DEBIT (−)	✔ T	FEE IF ANY (−)	DEPOSIT/CREDIT (+)	BALANCE	
	2/1	deposit/sales				763.21	763	21
	2/3	pay out/salary	176.59				763	21
							176	59
	2/5	pay/paint	298.04				586	62
							298	04
							288	58

124

Test 3. Lessons 11–15

1. $60
2. $1,940
3. $8
4. $392
5. $5.81
6. $284.69
7. $82.60
8. $468.05
9. $23.40
10. $444.65
11. $1,578.01
12. $6,086.61
13. $3,642.97
14. $10,648.69
15. 53%
16. $71.54
17. 23.5%
18. 33.3%
19. 15.3%
20. 27.9%
21. Pie chart
22. $10.34
23. $30.42
24. $46.55
25. $463.94

Test 4. Lessons 16–20

1. $8,500
2. 24.5%
3. ($3,600)
4. (12.4%)
5. $9,563.40
6. 7,286.40
7. $3,870.90
8. $2,277.00
9. ($2,660)
10. (11.08%)
11. 14,290
12. 34%
13. $800
14. $5,800
15. $2,945
16. $15,345
17. $12.05
18. $579.53
19. $526.28
20. $47,171.19
21. 10 years
22. 10%
23. $400
24. $2,400
25. $100

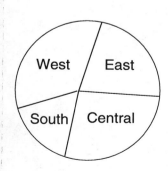

Test 5. Lesson 21–23

7. ___$2,000___

8. ___$25,800___

9. ___$24,260___

10. ___0___

20. Assets = Liabilities + Owner's Equity

21. right

22. liability

23. things of value belonging to a business

24. cash

25. balance sheet

BILL'S CLOTHING STORE
INCOME STATEMENT
For the Quarter Ended December 199–

			Percent of Net Sales
Revenue:			
Sales	203,700		
Less: Returns	7,340		
Net sales		196,360	
Cost of goods sold:			
Merchandise Inventory, Jan. 1	23,500		1. _11.54_
Purchases	140,200		2. _68.83_
COG available for sale, Jan. 1	163,700		3. _80.36_
Less: Mdse Inv., Dec. 31	18,210		4. _8.94_
Cost of goods sold		145,490	5. _7.10_
Gross profit		50,870	6. _24.97_

_____ NO. _____

	DATE	EXPLANATION	POST REF.	DEBIT	CREDIT	BALANCE	
						DEBIT	CREDIT
11.						4000 –	
12.						3250 –	
13.						1350	
14.						3850	

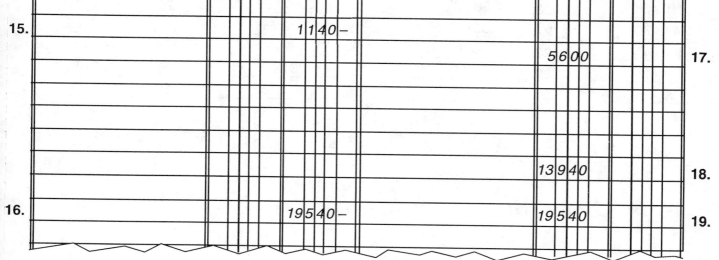

15.			1140 –				
					5600		**17.**
					13940		**18.**
16.			19540 –		19540		**19.**

Supp. Touch Drill 1

1. 789
2. 2,148
3. 1,662
4. 1,779
5. 128,719
6. 324,274
7. 154,122
8. 307,923
9. 13,326
10. 65,861
11. 5,776
12. 20,807
13. 380,171
14. 248,569
15. 36,493
16. 309,022
17. 310.75
18. 397.63
19. 11,988.33
20. 4,548.35
21. 1,204.76
22. 137,180.85
23. 1,089.28
24. 1,934.79
25. 838.84
26. 910.45
27. 1,493.70
28. 399.37
29. 787.82
30. 390.47

Supp. Touch Drill 2

1. 1,080
2. 1,554
3. 2,786
4. 1,860
5. 167,409
6. 172,665
7. 54,139
8. 151,403
9. 43,226
10. 36,099
11. 22,786
12. 38,593
13. 348,471
14. 278,569
15. 235,633
16. 241,181
17. 109,505
18. 4,214
19. 5,280
20. 134,000
21. 17,138
22. 47,222,006
23. 1,215.35
24. 1,952.59
25. 838.84
26. 2,381.35
27. 1,001.75
28. 390.88
29. 362.80
30. 233.70

Supp. Touch Drill 3

1. 2,130
2. 2,351
3. 1,544
4. 2,805
5. 198,657
6. 215,961
7. 298,139
8. 123,183
9. 57,216
10. 9,183
11. 18,781
12. 33,571
13. 406,513
14. 298,099
15. 96,633
16. 761,097
17. 8,645
18. 846
19. 1,920
20. 522,000
21. 1,435
22. 16,606
23. 526.02
24. 2,601.58
25. 918.46
26. 2,600.69
27. 802.75
28. 129.66
29. 261.88
30. 128.78

Supp. Touch Drill 4

1. 2,220
2. 2,896
3. 2,219
4. 2,209
5. 250,115
6. 134,801
7. 221,190
8. 137,103
9. 61,166
10. 5,179
11. 11,481
12. 13,631
13. 489,483
14. 118,079
15. 76,543
16. 431,393
17. 1,995
18. 611
19. 2,160
20. 6,300
21. 3,355
22. 3,476
23. 463.44
24. 2,927.77
25. 990.56
26. 1,170.65
27. 1,162.75
28. 140.76
29. 151.38
30. 237.53

Comprehensive Final Test (Lessons 1-23)

1.	3,523	26.	$100
2.	2,895	27.	$4,900
3.	2,958	28.	$10.50
4.	1,488	29.	$339.50
5.	2,943	30.	$1.71
6.	17.84	31.	$168.97
7.	18.30	32.	$1504.38
8.	15.02	33.	$5,265.33
9.	15.92	34.	$290.61
10.	23.54	35.	$1198.77
11.	7.3	36.	$16.18
12.	21.8	37.	$45.71
13.	3.8	38.	$53.80
14.	19.6	39.	$526.31
15.	10.0	40.	$1,260
16.	$105.64	41.	$8,260
17.	$43.46	42.	$1,776.50
18.	$58.29	43.	$5576.50
19.	$50.40	44.	$10.65
20.	$257.79	45.	$321.47
21.	10%	46.	$65,000
22.	3/20	47.	$296,300
23.	15%	48.	$5,870
24.	3/4		
25.	0.75		

49. The Income Statement

50. The Balance Sheet